The Gift of Joy

LESLIE B. FLYNN

While this book is designed for the reader's personal use and profit, it is also intended for group study. A Leader's Guide is available from your local bookstore or from the publisher at $2.50.

VICTOR BOOKS

a division of SP Publications, Inc.

WHEATON, ILLINOIS 60187

Offices also in Fullerton, California • Whitby, Ontario, Canada • Amersham-on-the-Hill, Bucks, England

Unless otherwise noted, Scripture quotations are from the King
James Version. Other quotations are from *The New International
Version* (NIV), © 1973, The New York Bible Society; *The Living
Bible* (LB), © Tyndale House Publishers, Wheaton, Illinois. All
quotations used by permission.

Recommended Dewey Decimal Classification: 248
Suggested Subject Headings: CHRISTIAN LIFE; SPIRITUAL LIFE

Library of Congress Catalog Card Number: 79-67851
ISBN: 0-88207-794-5

VICTOR BOOKS
A division of SP Publications, Inc.
P.O. Box 1825 • Wheaton, Illinois 60187

To
Bernice, my wife,
my seven daughters,
my grandchildren,
my in-laws,
my cousins,
all from whom I have received
the joy of family.

Contents

1 Just What Is Joy?

A national magazine featured a picture without a caption. It showed a group of well-fed, well-dressed, and apparently well-to-do men and women all staring at the same thing.

But every face displayed anxiety, fear, or unhappiness. Not one smiling countenance graced the 20 or so faces. It seemed that some tragedy had grabbed their attention. Since the photo's background indicated a city street, perhaps a traffic accident with a seriously injured victim was the focus of their concern. What was the disaster confronting them?

The answer was surprisingly simple. A newspaper photographer, on his way to an assignment, came to a busy, downtown intersection. Waiting to cross the crowded street, he was struck by the expressions on the faces of those on the opposite side of the street, also waiting to cross.

They were merely waiting for the red traffic light to turn green. The unhappiness on their faces was personal, coming from within them, not from any tragedy before their eyes. Though their dress reflected prosperity, their faces mirrored the unhappiness of inner poverty.

It is so easy for us to associate the sunny, smiling face with the shallow, superficial disposition, and to link the melancholy countenance with deep piety. Joy is often considered by many to be a satanic instrument, and gloom, a divine characteristic.

Some people think joy is unspeakable, and that it defies definition. They refer to speechless joy, because all words to describe joy are inadequate. They claim joy is a matter of experience rather than analysis, of intuition, rather than definition. How can you define a sunset for a blind man, or the scent of lilacs for a person with no sense of smell?

Others hesitate to define joy, afraid that it will lose its wonder in the process—like a lovely flower when it is dissected petal by petal. But an understanding of the nature of joy will give us a greater appreciation of joy.

A State of Exultation
In general, joy is the emotion evoked by a pleasurable experience or prospect. A wealth of synonymns are often used to describe it: bliss, buoyancy, cheerfulness, delight, ecstasy, elation, exuberance, felicity, gaiety, gladness, glee, hilarity, jubilation, rapture, rejoicing. The range of these words indicates that the thrill of joy may come with varying intensity, from serene joy to ebullient joy.

But let's define the deep-down exultation which transcends common delights. This kind of joy flows from God's special grace and is experienced by believers only. The psalmist declared that God-implanted gladness excels the elation at a full harvest (Ps. 4:7). It is this genuine joy that can make the Christian soul calmly hum a gloria or enthusiastically shout a hallelujah.

Fruit of the Spirit

Christian joy is a fruit of the Holy Spirit, one of that lovely cluster of Christlike characteristics enumerated by Paul (Gal. 5:22). In fact, joy is listed second, immediately following love.

Because it is produced by the Spirit within, joy cannot be manufactured by outside forces. This joy is also to be differentiated from a lighthearted disposition.

Laughter is not joy. A generation ago a religious sect in Hungary believed that salvation could be gained by laughter. When some of the group put their doctrine into practice, they were arrested as public nuisances.

Ecstatic hilarity is not a proper biblical concept of Christianity. But inner delight may sometimes lead to outer laughter. A popular Bible teacher I once knew was publicly rebuked at a Bible conference for indulging in what some straight-laced people considered to be too much humor. His reply was, "When I got saved, I got the joy of the Lord. I can't help it if it runs over."

Merriment is not joy. People indulging in noisy hilarity are not necessarily joyful. Many depressed individuals possess what is known as a smiling depression, because they smile to cover up inner sadness.

A despondent man asked a doctor for a cure for his blues. The doctor suggested an amusing book. "I've tried that and it hasn't worked," replied the patient. Then the doctor suggested a lively concert. But that had been tried too.

Finally the doctor said, "I've only one more suggestion, and if this doesn't work, I don't know what will. That new circus in town has a clown who keeps the audiences in stitches. If he can't drive away your blues, I don't know who can."

Replied the man, "I am that clown."

Too often the loudest laugh hides the hollowest heart. "Even in laughter the heart is sorrowful; and the end of that mirth is heaviness" (Prov. 14:13).

Joviality is not joy. Some people may naturally possess a bubbly, jovial personality, whereas others people may be melancholic and moody. We may be jovial because things are going our way, promising a rosy future. But like a flash, the smile may disappear and the heart swoon. Joviality, like happiness, is closely related to circumstances.

Happiness is not joy. Happiness depends on what happens, whereas Holy Spirit joy is independent of circumstances. Ocean gales, ripping across the Atlantic, can catapult waves 50 feet high. Yet 50 feet below, the water is perfectly calm. Happiness is like the surface of the sea—ever changing. Joy is like the ocean bed—ever the same.

To be happy all the time is an impossible task. Every person will face unhappy circumstances, but joy will still abide. We are pressed in on every side and perplexed. But like Paul, we can rejoice because we know that God never abandons us.

Wicked Haman happily headed home because of his invitation to dine with Queen Esther. But his delight was cut short when he spotted Mordecai, the Jew who never bowed to him (Es. 5:9). How different from Paul and Silas—who at midnight, with feet in stocks in the Philippian jail—sang joyfully to God.

Superior to laughter, merriment, joviality, and happiness, joy is that abiding exuberance of God's Spirit in man: "good measure, pressed down, and shaken together, and running over" (Luke 6:38). Joy has been called a foretaste of that face-to-face communion with God which will be rapturous through eternity.

A By-Product

The happiest people are generally those too busy to ask themselves, "Am I happy?" Absorbed in worthwhile activities, they don't have time to question their own personal happiness. When a person seeks happiness, it eludes him; but when he isn't looking for happiness, he finds it.

Likewise, the search for joy is futile. He who makes joy his goal is bound to fail. Joy is not something you strive for like an "A" in history, or an 80 in golf. We don't find joy; it finds us.

In fact, C.S. Lewis said that the subject of joy lost much interest for him after he became a Christian. Previously, the yearning for joy was a sort of pointer to the need for a visionary gleam. When he experienced Christian joy, the pointer lost its value, just as signposts are not the object of concentration once you've found the right road.

William Blake wrote,

> He who bends to himself a joy
> Doth the winged life destroy;
> But he who kisses the joy as it flies,
> Lives in eternity's sunrise.

What is true of the search for temporary happiness is also true of the search for genuine joy. Holy Spirit joy is a by-product of a right relationship with Jesus Christ. Not just the *thrill* of knowing Christ should be the believer's goal, but also the *knowing* of Christ. From this bond with Christ, joy will tag along as a side effect. By resting in Christ, and losing our lives in Him, we find joy.

A Right Relationship with Christ

Joy has been called the ecstasy of eternity in a soul that has made peace with God and is ready to do His will. A right relationship with Christ involves both being and doing, both standing before Him and serving Him. Joy results from a genuine spiritual commitment. It is the inner reality which produces an outer radiance.

The 400-year-old Heidelberg Catechism asks: "Question: What is your only comfort in life and in death?

Answer: That I belong—body and soul, in life and in death—not to myself, but to my faithful Saviour, Jesus Christ, who at the cost of His own blood has fully paid for all my sins.

Question: What comfort does the return of Christ give you?

Answer: That in all affliction and persecution, I may await with head high the very Judge from heaven who . . . shall take me, together with all His elect, to Himself into heavenly joy and glory."

According to the Harvard Research Center, directed by sociologist Dr. Pitirim Sorokin, a love-thy-neighbor attitude is the most essential ingredient in achieving happiness on the natural plane. Dr. Sorokin believes that self-centeredness and unhappiness go hand in hand.

Joy comes when we fulfill our duties. "If you know these things, happy are you if you do them," said Jesus (John 13:17). A missionary doctor, when asked if he was underpaid, replied, "Is there any greater remuneration then the simple thanks of a mother for whom you have just delivered the first living child in 13 pregnancies? Or the gratitude of a blind man who left your hospital seeing the path himself for the first time in many years? Or the joyful radiance on the face of a man who just received Christ as his Saviour—a man who will die within a few months from an inoperable cancer?"

A familiar acrostic spells joy:

> J—Jesus first
> O—Others second
> Y—Yourself last

Fulfillment toward the Father

On a secular level, happiness comes from a sense of fulfillment. When a baby handles a new object, inspecting it, putting it into things, putting things into it, and becoming absorbed with it, the baby derives a certain sense of satisfaction. When a couple become parents, they experience the joy of fulfillment.

Psychological fulfillment comes with sensory

awareness, logical thinking, confidence in our worth, assurance that we are loved and accepted, and faith in our competence to handle problems as they arise.

Social fulfillment comes when interpersonal relationships are handled properly. Intellectual satisfaction follows the solving of puzzles and the mastery of information.

Similarly, spiritual fulfillment (joy) comes when the mystery of life is solved; so that our identity problem is resolved, and we discover why we are here, where we came from, and where we are going. The harmonizing of himself with the rest of the created world, the process that led him from atheism to Christianity, C.S. Lewis called joy.

Man longs to regain the lost rapture present in Eden before the Fall—a yearning which no natural happiness can satisfy. Then, through divine revelation, the rapture returns. We understand that man was made in God's image, but fell through sin. We realize that we were born with a bent to sin, and out of tune with God. We also learn that we are the objects of God's love, who sent His Son to reconcile us to Himself. We recognize that through faith in Christ's mediatory work, we are adopted into God's family, thus becoming children of the King of kings. Furthermore, that we are here to serve Him through our gifts and opportunities, and that some day, at life's end, we shall go to live with Him forever.

Joy comes when we see our world-view as no longer fragmented, but rather, as integrated and unified. With the pieces fitting together in the jigsaw puzzle of life, we believe we have glimpsed the essence of the universe, the secret of things, as though a covering had been pulled aside. We don't understand everything, but we understand enough. At peace with our Maker, we then can live at peace with ourselves.

Significantly, one of the highest suicide rates is among psychiatrists. Many of them feel that they are the last resort when it comes to piecing life together for others—and if they don't have the answers, who does? Thus, despair takes over.

But God has the answers. He gives peace to those who turn to Him. Note the involvement of all three Persons in the Trinity. Joy is deep-down exultation, the fruit of the Spirit, a by-product of a right relationship with Christ, and a strong sense of fulfillment toward the Father.

More simply, joy is a glad-hearted quality of life with its roots deep in God. It is being overwhelmed with God.

2 Sad Faces

Ever since man was expelled from Eden there has been a shortage of joy. Dr. Vernon Grounds says, "Joy is about as rare as the bald eagle." Samuel Johnson once remarked that the human race is a vast assemblage of individuals who are counterfeiting happiness. Unfortunately, people of all ages are affected.

All Ages
About every 20 minutes someone in the United States commits suicide. World wide, half a million suicides are reported annually (Frank B. Minirth and Paul D. Meier, *Happiness Is a Choice*, Baker, 1978, p. 31). In 1964, the *New York Times* estimated that about 5 million people then living in America had tried to kill themselves.

Unhappiness extends to all ages.

Many young people are unhappy. Suicide is the second leading cause of death among college students. But young people are not the only ones who are prone to suicide. Elderly people account for one quarter of reported suicides.

Many middle-aged people also exist without joy. Realizing that they will never reach their goals, their lives seem like reruns of a television program. One couple wrote to a syndicated columnist, "We have a nice home, well-furnished; a new car, and money in the bank. Our two sons have finished college and are happily married and doing well. We have excellent jobs and our combined incomes make it possible for us to live comfortably. So why are we writing this letter? Because suddenly, we find life empty and boring. Are we different, or does this happen to all couples in later midlife?"

Elusive Happiness

Is everybody unhappy?

In His kindness to mankind, even nonbelievers, God has given a measure of happiness to all. Most people have experienced happiness to some degree at some time. But happiness is relative. What may be pleasure to one may be pain to another. What may bring pleasure to the body may not grant happiness to the mind. The law of diminishing returns makes the second piece of cake less satisfying than the first, the third piece even less so.

Many young people today have too much too soon. By high school some are already bored by the usual pleasures, so they seek greater excitement in drugs, perversion, or violence. Their "fulfillment" comes from trying everything that turns them on. Letdown is guaranteed—the increasing thrills have to end sometime. The "high" won't last forever.

Even minor letdowns after exciting weekends may diminish happiness. Organizations for suicide prevention claim Monday and Tuesday as their busiest days—as well as nighttime, holidays, and post-holiday periods. Interestingly, the suicide rate rises during economic depression for "happiness" has taken wings and flown away.

Night Questions

Pollution, nuclear armaments, the population explosion, and the energy crisis all add to the gloom over our world situation. Man's tranquility is disturbed not only by the problem of his future, but also by questions concerning his origin and purpose. "Where did I come from? Why am I here? Where am I going?" have been called "night questions." In the wee hours of the morning, when silence gives us time to face reality, these questions invade our minds. Until these are satisfactorily answered, we cannot know genuine joy.

Two Dallas-based psychiatrists, after years of research, affirm "with a deep inner conviction that a majority of human beings do *not* have inner peace and joy" (Minirth and Meier, *Happiness Is a Choice*, p. 12).

These psychiatrists also point out that depression is America's number one health problem. "A majority of Americans suffer from a serious, clinical depression sometime during their lives. At the present time, 1 American in 20 is medically diagnosed as suffering from depression. Of course, many, many more are depressed but never receive help. According to 1 estimate about 20 million persons in America between the ages of 18 and 74 are currently depressed" (Ibid., p. 20).

As St. Augustine put it, "Man was made for God and will not rest until he rests in God." Till man finds divine satisfaction, he will remain basically unhappy and unfulfilled, wistfully sighing for a long-missing note.

Unhappy Christians

Many professing Christians are miserable. Though for a short time after their conversion they were extremely happy, radiance soon retreated. Now and again a little sliver of joy is retrieved at some moving worship service or revival meeting. But these happy flashes are short-lived; so they spend much time searching for spiritual satisfaction.

Perhaps sadness, is often equated with spirituality because of the solemnity of earlier church leaders.

Even today, many people associate church with a certain grimness. People don uncomfortable garb, work themselves into a joyless frame of mind, then betake themselves into a severe, barnlike building with hard pews and an austere atmosphere.

One Easter Sunday morning a television network carried the worship service of a large, Protestant congregation. The preacher related the amazing story of the empty tomb. Enthusiastically, he recited the dividends that issue from the Resurrection. Though nothing was wrong with the preacher's message, according to one observer, "Something was strange." It was the deadpan look on the faces of the congregation. Not a radiant face among hundreds. Blank, bothered, bored countenances, but not glowing with resurrection glory.

Happily, in recent years more emphasis has been placed on worship as joyful celebration. But, unfortunately, in many instances the soul's exultation is confined to the sanctuary's four walls. A little girl, noting the change in the people leaving a morning service, asked, "Mother, where did the Christians put all that joy they were singing about?"

Is There an Answer?

Unfortunately to many, sadness and sanctity are synonymous. Charles Haddon Spurgeon received a letter from a church visitor. The man told Spurgeon that as soon as he entered the church, he felt it could not be the house of God. First, the crowd was too large—the narrow way that leads to life is found by few. Also, Spurgeon looked too cheerful. And when the visitor saw the happy faces in the congregation, he thought, *"These people know nothing about the depravity of their hearts, or the inward struggles of believers."*

This man then moved on to a small chapel where the minister looked as though he had been in the furnace of affliction. The eight persons present seemed so depressed that he felt quite at home. Spurgeon commented, "I suppose he sat down and sang,

> My willing soul would stay
> In such a frame as this,
> And sit and sing herself away
> From everything like bliss."

Though Spurgeon's congregation had happy faces, many worshipers do not. Vance Havner put it, "The average Sunday morning congregation appears as if it has gathered to mourn a defeat rather than celebrate a victory. Too many seem to be enduring their salvation, instead of enjoying it. We need to remind ourselves that we've not been called to a funeral, but to a feast!"

A masterful piece of satanic propaganda declares that dolor denotes devotion, and delight spells depravity. Even some believers who testify they have been preserved look more like they have been pickled. A song leader who couldn't get the congregation to sing, paused between stanzas, pointed to an unco-operative man, and said, "Will you please stand, sir, and lead us in a frown?"

The Father Is Joyful

Wrongly do we think of God as rigid, impassive, sad, and stern. As the manufacturer of the oil of gladness, as well as of every good and perfect gift, He has within Himself all the fullness of bliss. The deep, broad, pure rivers of blessedness, which flow in every direction from heaven's domain, originate in Him in whom are not only all the treasures of wisdom, truth, and goodness, but of joy as well.

Commenting on Paul's declaration that God "is the blessed and only Potentate" (1 Tim. 6:15), Vernon Grounds says, "Since blessed means happy, Paul is here affirming that God is happy. The happy God! God in Himself is a shoreless sea of vibrant glory, a fathomless ocean of sheerest ecstasy. . . . God Himself is the Rejoicer who before the hosts of heaven reacts with a thrilling happiness that baffles the language and logic of earth. Infinitely joyful, He is the Source of all genuine joy."

God is not a heavenly Scrooge, a celestial kill-joy determined to keep His children from a good time. God is described as rejoicing in the prosperity of His people, and in His own works (Deut. 30:9; Ps. 104:31). He breaks forth in singing (Zeph. 3:17). God is not only a comfort; He is a joy! Just as the Bible says, "God is love," it could as truthfully say, "God is joy."

The Old Testament Enjoins Joy

A preacher doing spadework for a sermon on joy turned to a concordance and found so many entries under the headings of joy, joyful, and rejoice that he concluded no one could call Christianity a religion of sadness. Of the more than 400 references, by far more than half are in the Old Testament.

Nature. After each creative act, God saw "that it was good." He derived quiet joy from all of nature—inanimate, animalistic, and human. Nature is to exult in its Creator. God rightfully deserves our praise, not only for His marvelous works, but also for who He is.

Incidentally, God has so constituted us to make it for us easier to be joyful. Psychologists say that we tend to forget the unpleasant, and to remember more easily the delightful. Even our memories thus contribute to our joy.

Feasts. Israel's holy days were also holidays. The three annual feasts at Jerusalem—Passover, First-fruits, and Tabernacles—involved times of joy, for they were social as well as solemn gatherings.

The silver trumpets were to be blown on solemn days but also "in the day of your gladness" (Num. 10:10). The title for the fiftieth year, *jubilee*, indicated a joyous occasion, because this year of liberty permitted every man to regain his freedom and possessions (Lev. 25:8-24). When Passover was revived in Hezekiah's reign, it brought a surge of great joy, unsurpassed since Solomon's day (2 Chron. 30:21, 23, 26).

Temple. Organized singing and instrumentation were part of temple worship in David's day. Groups of Levites were assigned to perform this ministry. Among the returning remnant under Zerubbabel were 200 singing men and women (Ezra 2:65). When the temple order was restored in Nehemiah's time, again singers accompanied by cymbals, psalteries, and harps, lifted songs of praise and thanksgiving to God (1 Chron. 25:1-7; Neh. 12:27-28, 45-47).

Psalms. The worship of Israel was an invitation to joy. "O come, let us sing, let us make a joyful noise" (95:1-2). "But let all those that put their trust in Thee rejoice; let them ever shout for joy" (5:11).

Psalm 100 begins, "Make a joyful noise unto the Lord, all ye lands. Serve the Lord with gladness; come before His presence with singing" (vv. 1-2).

The Old Testament breathes the atmosphere of joy, as the command to praise God is repeated over and over, because of His greatness, His glory, and His goodness.

Joy in the New Testament

We do the Lord Jesus an injustice if we paint Him as a melancholy man, for He was indeed more glad than sad. We will focus on the joy of Jesus later in this book.

Though the Gospel's focus was on a cruel cross, and

though the early church was soaked in martyrs' blood,
a quick scan of the Book of Acts highlights a jubilant,
victorious people.

In those early, post-Pentecost days, believers ate
their meat with gladness and praise (Acts 2:46-47).
The healed lame man entered the temple, leaping
and praising God (3:9). Philip's preaching in Samaria
brought great joy to that city (8:8). If we follow Paul
from prison to prison, from privation to privation, we
find him glorying in tribulation, rejoicing in sorrow,
and singing praises in jail at midnight.

Epistles. Paul testified that "we also joy in God
through our Lord Jesus Christ" (Rom. 5:11). Later, he
prayed that the God of peace would fill the Romans
"with all joy and peace in believing" (15:13). The
Book of Philippians has been called "the epistle of
joy" because of its 17 or so references to that topic.

Peter delighted in a "joy unspeakable and full of
glory" (1 Peter 1:8). John wrote his first epistle so that
its recipients might have full joy (1 John 1:4).

Revelation. The final book of the Bible is a volume
of joy because of its recurrent theme of victory. The
songs magnify the power of God in creation, judgment, and redemption. Enemies are defeated. Mar-
tyred saints overcome hunger, heat, night, and tears.
Joy floods the gates of heaven.

The Bible ends with choirs of redeemed sinners
vibrantly singing their glad thanksgiving, "And I
heard as it were the voice of a great multitude . . .
saying, 'Alleluia; for the Lord God omnipotent reign-
eth.' Let us be glad and rejoice, and give honor to
Him; for the marriage of the Lamb is come, and His
wife hath made herself ready" (Rev. 19:6-7). The Gos-

pel is both a message of joy, and an invitation to commence a life of joy.

The Command to Be Joyful

All idea of gloom, as a characteristic of the Christian life, is dispelled by Paul's order to the Philippians, "Rejoice in the Lord" (Phil. 3:1). The language is imperative. As though some doubted the possibility of obedience in daily living, Paul deliberately added, "and again I say, rejoice" (4:4).

The shortest verse in the Greek text is a command to gladness, "Rejoice evermore" (1 Thes. 5:16). "Be of good cheer" occurs only in the imperative in the New Testament.

In A.D. 200, Cyprian, Bishop of Carthage, wrote to a friend about the in-depth joy of early believers. "This is a cheerful world as I see it from my fair garden. . . . But if I could ascend some high mountain and look out over the wide lands, you know very well what I would see. Brigands on the highways. Pirates on the seas. Armies fighting. Cities burning. In the amphitheatres men murdered to please applauding crowds. Selfishness and cruelty, and misery and despair, under all roofs. It is a bad world, Donatus, an incredibly bad world. But I have discovered in the midst of it, a quiet and holy people who have learned a great secret. They have found a joy which is a thousand times better than that of any of the pleasures of our sinful life. They are despised and persecuted, but they care not. They are masters of their souls. They have overcome the world. These people, Donatus, are Christians, and I am one of them" (G. Ernest Thomas, *What Jesus Was Like*, Pulpit Press, 1946, p.

63-64). Cyprian had found true joy.

We know that the final message about life is not the sordid, morbid headlines of nightly newspapers. The last word is victory.

Godliness is not gloom, but gladness. A Sunday morning prayer in the *Book of Common Prayer* states, "May thy chosen people be joyful."

But where can joy be found? Are people looking in the right place?

3 Where Can Joy Be Found?

Mischievous boys broke into a department store one night and switched price tags on the items. Television sets became 2¢ per pound. Bicycles, 29¢ each. Mink coats were marked for $2.98. Nails soared to $79.95 a piece. Wastebaskets were priced at $1500.

Isn't this a parable of life? People often pursue goods and goals of little worth, neglecting matters of real value.

Take Ernest Hemingway for example. His biographer was perplexed by the writer's suicide. In the foreword, the biographer listed what Hemingway had going for him: He had won both the Nobel and Pulitzer Prizes; he had a home in Idaho's Sawtooth Mountains; an apartment in New York; a specially rigged yacht to fish the Gulf Stream; apartments available at the Ritz in Paris and at the Gritti in Venice; a sturdy marriage; and fine friends everywhere. Yet in 1961, this literary genius put a shotgun to his head and

27

killed himself. The biographer, though Hemingway's close friend for 14 years, admitted he did not know why (A.E. Hotchner, *Papa Hemingway*, Random House, 1966).

How many people have tasted success and prosperity, yet know only emptiness of spirit? Where do people look for joy?

In Riches
People often reason, "If I had money, land, stocks and bonds, three cars, a swimming pool, a boat, and a plane, *then* I'd be happy."

The poor think that if they struck it rich, they would be joyful. The rich *know* this isn't so. Millionaire Jay Gould said, when dying, "I suppose I am the most miserable man on earth." Steel magnate Andrew Carnegie remarked, "Millionaires seldom smile and never laugh."

Paul warned Timothy that the love of money is the root of all evil (1 Tim. 6:10). James also urged believers not to treasure their riches because their wealth was not eternal (James 5:1-5).

In Pleasure
Here's a man who lives it up. People envy his lifestyle. But is he happy? He's not sure. Often on the morning after the night before, his mouth tastes like rotten wood, his head feels like exploding, and his liver rebukes him. Afraid to look into the mirror too closely, he dives again into another round of sensual gratification. Far from experiencing joy, he's really disgusted with himself.

Pleasure has its proper place, when rationally controlled. Even sinful delights yield a degree of pleasure (Heb. 11:25). But these are short-lived, disappointing, and limited. Hedonism with its "eat, drink, and be merry" philosophy leads to the dead-end street of frustration, boredom, and burned-out ashes. Robert Burns wrote,

> Pleasures are as poppies spread;
> You seize the flower, the bloom is shed.

Lord Chesterton said, "I have run the silly rounds of pleasure, and by no means desire to repeat the nauseous dose." The woman at the well, after affairs with six men, was still seeking the Living Water of genuine joy (John 4:18, 39). But Peter had the answer. He exhorted believers to live according to God's will, and forsake those evil pleasures sought before knowing God (1 Peter 4:2-5).

In Power

Many people think military conquest, position, or power can bring joy. Alexander the Great, who conquered the world of his day, wept because there were no more worlds to conquer.

In his early career Mussolini exclaimed, "I am obsessed by one wild desire. It consumes my whole being. I want to make a mark on my era with my will." Then with great fierceness he scratched the back of a chair, muttering, "like the claw of a lion." Later, Mussolini was executed without finding happiness.

Svetlana Stalin, after defecting to America, said of her dictator-father, "I believe that the conqueror himself was not happy at all. On the contrary, there came complete loneliness, unhappiness, disappointment and suspicion in all around him."

Sir Winston Churchill, according to the *New York Times*, uttered as his last sentence, "I am bored with it all." Even in the Bible, everyone who heard the Gospel did not accept it. King Agrippa's response to Paul's testimony was, "Almost thou persuadest me to be a Christian" (Acts 26:28).

In Fame

Lord Beaconsfield (Disraeli), who enjoyed more than his share of fame as prime minister of England, wrote, "Youth is a mistake; manhood, a struggle; old age, a regret."

Essayist Charles Lamb remarked, "I walk up and down thinking I am happy, and knowing I am not."

Many think, "If I could just have my name up in bright lights like a celebrity, then I would be happy." In 1978 Chris Evert, two-time Wimbledon women's tennis champion and winner of over a million dollars the previous year, took four months off from professional tennis because, according to the Associated Press, "She realized she was not happy."

God's Word warns against the selfish, conceited attitude. "Do not think of yourself more highly than you ought, but rather think of yourself with sober judgment" (Rom. 12:3, NIV). Later on, Paul wrote, "Don't be proud, but be willing to associate with people of low position. Don't be conceited" (v. 16, NIV).

In Drugs and Drink

"Of the thousands of [drug] addicts who have come to Teen Challenge," reports its director, Don Wilkerson, "not a single one has ever told us that he had found that deeper meaning through dope, or that drugs had given him the happiness, kicks, or thrills that he had sought. What's more, never have I heard of anyone anywhere who was happy that he had become addicted" (*The Gutter and the Ghetto*, Word, 1969, p. 168).

The manager of a special banquet room in a Japanese hotel noticed that no one was buying liquor. He turned to one of the guests. "Did you have cocktails before you came?" The guest, Dr. Donald Hoke, then president of Tokyo Bible College, answered no. Then the manager asked, "You mean you get happy on orange juice and ginger ale!"

Many think a party without drinks is dull. Though intoxicants temporarily stupefy, and drown out trouble, true joy is not imbibed from a bottle. This is why God commands believers to "behave decently, as in the daytime, not in orgies and drunkenness, not in sexual immorality, and debauchery, not in dissension and jealousy" (Rom. 13:3, NIV).

Solomon and Modern America

If ever a person was qualified to pass judgment on the ability of earthly goods and glory to satisfy the human heart, it was King Solomon. He tried mirth, magnificent mansions and estates, might, money, music, material possessions, and mistresses. He indulged in every pleasure and spared nothing to fill the emptiness of his life (Ecc. 2:1-9). "Whatsoever mine eyes desired I kept not from them, I withheld not my heart from any joy" (v. 10). But his conclusion was, "Behold, all was vanity and vexation of spirit". . . . Vanity of vanities . . . all is vanity" (2:11; 1:2). Modern psychology would call it *existential vacuum.*

Shakespeare's character in the historical tragedy *The Life and Death of King John* said,

There's nothing in this world can make me joy
Life is as tedious as a twice-told tale
Vexing the dull ear of a drowsy man
And bitter shame hath spoiled the sweet world's taste
That it yields naught but shame and bitterness.

Americans' prosperity has not brought happiness.

Never has a generation been bombarded by a more sophisticated network of media to eat more, play more, and have more fun. Someone called the U.S.A. the rich fool of Jesus' parable, swollen to the size of a nation. With our highest per capita income in the world, shining cars, stocked refrigerators, humming vacuum cleaners, noisy radios, color televisions, and roaring jets, large numbers of Americans have been able to indulge their whims on a scale unprecedented in history. Our citizens should be supremely happy, but instead are consuming greater quantities of sleeping pills and tranquilizers. The person who lives for instant gratification exists restlessly with unsatisfied desires.

An American was describing the glories of his country to an African leader. After a recital of America's industrial genius and material prosperity, the unimpressed African solemnly asked, "But are your people happy?"

It's Elusive

Our American constitution, vouchsafing life and liberty to us, could not guarantee happiness, but only the *pursuit* of happiness. In *Pilgrim's Regress*, C.S. Lewis describes joy as a longing for an unnameable something which pierces us like a sword. Sheldon Vanauken elaborates, "But, then, we fix that sweet and poignant longing for joy upon some earthly object. We shall, we believe, find that joy if only we can climb the blue mountains, find the blue flower, win the love of some particular lady in blue, or sail beyond the blue horizon in our schooner to our own new-found land. Secretly we are all perhaps the questing knight. And yet, whatever the object of our quest, we learn when we find it that it does not ever contain the joy that broke our heart with longing" (*A Severe Mercy*, Harper and Row, 1977, p. 207).

Trying to find satisfaction in the things of this world is like chasing soap bubbles, or trying to reach the pot of gold at the end of the rainbow. Happiness is like the line of the horizon. Though we chase after it our entire life, we'll never catch it. Thus all egocentric motivational goals are self-defeating. The Bible does not deny the valid enjoyment of pleasure, but the search for pleasure as the primary goal leads to futility. Unhappiness is not knowing what we crave, and spending our energies trying to get it.

Source of Joy
Where, then, can genuine joy be found?

A survey taken by the public relations firm of Batten, Barton, Durstine, & Osborne, indicated that religious people are "notably happier" than nonreligious ones. But more than religion is needed to bring real joy.

C.S. Lewis says that whatever we are longing for,

whether it be the "Island in the West" in *Pilgrim's Regress,* or climbing some mountain, or sailing some sea, these things will never fully bring joy, because what we are really longing for is God. And God can be known only through Jesus Christ.

Man cannot live by bread alone (nor money, fame, power, or pleasure). God designed salvation through Jesus Christ to satisfy the deepest longings of the human heart, and to give life abundant. This is why the Bible says, "Rejoice in the Lord" (Phil. 4:4). Malcolm Muggeridge, worldly wise, world famous ex-editor of *Punch,* said, "A man's effort to make himself personally and collectively happy in earthly terms is doomed to failure. He must indeed, as Christ said, be born again, be a new man, or he's nothing. So at least I have concluded, having failed to find in past experiences, present dilemmas or future expectations, any alternative proposition."

The Jesus movement was spawned from the failure of things to satisfy the restlessness of the youth culture of the 60s. When young people rejected the joyless lifestyle of their materialistic parents, they sought reality in drugs. When chemical highs didn't bring lasting happiness, this void provided fertile soil for the Gospel and its joy.

Billy Graham's mother wrote, "Upon what do we depend for our happiness? Is it bright sunshine and clear skies? No. Fine clothes and lovely homes? No. Is it money? Is it fun? No. Fun is a passing experience and does not always express joy. Joy, for the Christian, is the result of an inward sense of peace which comes from a right relationship with God. Our first joy is the consciousness that Christ is ours. Homes and houses don't create Christian happiness. Christ has to bring it" (Morrow Coffey Graham, *Decision*, May 1972).

It is in Christ that we have our inheritance, in Him that we are blessed with all spiritual blessings, in Him that we have redemption through His blood. Therefore, it is in Christ that we are to rejoice—not in spiritual gifts, nor in opportunities for service, nor in growth in grace. Joy belongs to him who finds fulfillment in Christ. So often we cannot rejoice in circumstances, but we can rejoice in Him.

On a train from Kansas City to Chicago during World War II a woman, traveling without her evangelist-husband, was unable to find a seat. The conductor said, "I'm going to put you in with two other women."

One was a giddy, young blond with a heavily painted face, gaudy dress, filthy vocabulary, and a small bottle of whiskey in her coat pocket. The other was a well-dressed lady of culture and refinement whose husband was a prominent businessman.

Though the ride was long and the compartment small, the women talked freely. The giddy blond offered the other two a drink, which they refused. She told how she would spend the weekend with a soldier in Chicago, and how she lived for pleasure. Then she tried on the distinguished lady's large diamond rings, exclaiming how happy she would be if she had such jewelry and a mink coat. The evangelist's wife told of her life married to a preacher, and how happy she was to be a Christian and in the Lord's work.

The well-dressed woman then spoke to the blond. "My dear, you say you would be the happiest woman in the world if only you had my rings, my mink, and my home. I have these and a great many more things. But instead of being happy, I believe I am the unhappiest woman in the world. I have wealth, a large home, servants and expensive cars, but for years I've not been happy. My husband and I have drifted apart; our love has grown cold. From our conversation today, I have found where the trouble lies. I have left Christ out of my life, and so have you. The evangelist's wife has found the secret of a happy life, the Lord Jesus Christ." The Gospel song sums it up:

> I cried to broken cisterns, Lord,
> But, ah, the waters failed;
> E'en as I stooped to drink, they fled
> And mocked me as I wailed.
>
> Now none but Christ can satisfy,
> None other name but His;
> There's love and life and lasting joy,
> Lord Jesus, found in Thee.

Though Christ is the source of true, deep-down joy, are there not some delights open to the non-Christian? Are there such things as common joys?

4 Common Joys

A man was invited to spend the weekend at an old friend's country home. The host pointed out the lovely view from his living-room picture window, "See the mountains, the valleys, the winding river!" His guest, a rather rigid Christian, replied, "How can a heavenly man take pleasure in an earthly view?"

Later at dinner, the host served a dish of delicious peaches and cream. When his guest asked for a second helping, the host graciously obliged, then asked, "How can a heavenly man take pleasure in earthly things like peaches and cream?"

The truth is, God has given us many earthly things to enjoy. Theologians speak of *common grace* and *special grace*. By common grace God grants many favors to all mankind, whether regenerate or unregenerate (Matt. 5:45). Through special grace God gives salvation and a host of spiritual blessings. Among common kindnesses available are sunshine, rain, and happy marriages. Also included are the common delights of life.

Common joy, which may be enjoyed by all persons, should be distinguished from *genuine* joy. Genuine joy is produced through God's special grace as a fruit of the Spirit, and reserved for believers only.

But now let's look at some major sources of common joy.

Nature

The Lord made "to grow every tree that is pleasant to the sight" (Gen. 2:9). The Lord made the song of the bird, the fragrance of the lilac, snow-peaked mountains, the ocean with its endless swells, the richly colored sunset, waving wheat fields, the variety of animals, and the shining stars. The poet speaks of creation "where every prospect pleases and only man is vile."

Judaism shows a profound appreciation of nature. The trees in bloom and the fragrance of flowers should not go unnoticed. Even the physical charms of womanhood are the handiwork of God, not the lure of Satan. Recognizing these common joys should result in joyous thanksgiving to God.

News commentator Walter Cronkite, when asked how he relaxed, replied, "I go to the sea by a small boat. With one's vessel propelled by the same power of wind that moved the ancients, faced by the same challenges and beauty of nature, one can achieve, at least momentarily, some degree of serenity" (*Look*, 27 July 1971).

Scott Carpenter, second American to circle the earth in space, said, "The colors glowed vigorously alive with light. I watched the band of sunset narrow until nothing was left but a rim of blue. I felt the experience all but supernatural."

Family

A man whose wife passed away lamented, "What fun is it to get big orders in my business when I have no one at home to hear about them? What does money mean when I have no one to lavish it on? Rather, my success accentuates my loneliness. I would gladly give it all up, if I could have her back again."

No wonder the writer of the Book of Proverbs advises, "Rejoice with the wife of thy youth . . . and be thou ravished always with her love" (5:18-19). Isaac's bride, Rebekah, brought comfort to him after his mother's death (Gen. 24:67). Jacob so delighted in Rachel that his seven years of labor to earn her hand seemed but a few days (Gen. 29:20).

Parenthood also brings joy. The reactions of three biblical mothers prove this. At the birth of her first son Eve exclaimed, "I have gotten a man from the Lord" (Gen. 4:1). When barren Sarah finally bore a son, he was called Laughter (Isaac). After Samuel's birth Hannah praised, "My heart rejoiceth in the Lord" (1 Sam. 2:1).

In childbirth the pangs of labor are exchanged for the joys of motherhood. The psalmist said, "Lo, children are an heritage of the Lord; and the fruit of the womb is His reward. As arrows are in the hand of a mighty man; so are children of the youth. Happy is the man that hath his quiver full of them" (127:3-4).

C.S. Lewis thought that perhaps half of all the happiness in the world came from friendship genuinely generated among a few people, centered around a common interest (Clyde S. Kilby, *The Christian World of C.S. Lewis*, Eerdmans, 1964, p. 24).

Bill Moyer, onetime presidential press secretary, finds recovery of joy by taking his family to a remote retreat with one or more of the couples who are his closest friends. He says, "We usually talk of small and personal and sometimes silly things, and occasionally, weighty questions that only friends can discuss without pretention—and sometimes for hours we talk hardly at all, simply enjoying the comfortable silence that good friends share only with each other. We poke fun at one another's pomposities, compare notes on the incorrigible conduct of our children, relive cherished experiences from the past, and share dreams; and always the time passes too quickly. I find myself buoyed (*Look*, 27 July 1971).

You don't have to be a believer in Christ to consider your photo album of friends one of your prized possessions.

Work

For many, work is a bore; for others, a blessing. In the Bible we read of the joy of the harvest, the gratification of bountiful fruit and golden grain gained from diligent labor. Deep engrossment in daily toil can be stimulating. One artist so enjoyed his work that some days he thought he would die of satisfaction.

A sense of achievement brings joy. The mechanic who whistles after repairing a difficult motor, the workman who knocks himself out on the assembly line to make sure no bolt is missing, the housewife who keeps her home neat and her children clean, all may find delight. Creating a first-rate salad may be more rewarding than painting a second-rate picture. Coming late to a banquet, an obstetrician seemed particularly elated. "I just delivered my thousandth baby," he said.

Dr. A.H. Maslow, professor of psychology at Brandeis, said he never met a happy person who did not have a commitment to work. This joy is open to all, believers or unbelievers.

Possessions
Anthropologists have often criticized missionaries for allegedly spoiling the "happiness" of innocent, naive nationals in underdeveloped parts of the world by introducing Western products. But pollster George Gallup argued that people in less developed nations are quite unhappy because they are poor (*Evangelical Newsletter*, 14 January 1955, p. 1). Things do bring some joy.

Though possessions do not provide deep-down, permanent joy, they are a source of common joy. In the midst of his warning to the rich not to trust in their wealth, but to be rich in good works by sharing with the needy, Paul made a significant assertion. "God . . . giveth us richly all things to enjoy" (1 Tim. 6:17).

Made in the image of the Supreme Artist, we may rightfully appreciate works of art, beautiful china, and exquisite jewelry with proper stewardship. Keats wrote, "A thing of beauty is a joy forever."

Study
To solve a math problem, to become proficient in a foreign language, to understand a writer, to master a

skill, to memorize a poem, to comprehend a philosophy, to find insight into complex, current social issues, these make for satisfaction. *The Living Bible* paraphrases Proverbs 15:2: "A wise teacher makes learning a joy." Emerson said, "In the highest civilization the book is the highest joy."

Body and Health

The beating of the heart and the wonder of one's own aliveness brings an intensity of delight. Izaak Walton, 17th century author of *The Compleat Angler*, said, "Look to your health; and if you have it, praise God, and value it next to a good conscience; for health is the second blessing that we mortals are capable of; a blessing that money cannot buy."

A mistaken spirituality belittles the pleasures of the five senses. To relish anew the joy of taste and smell, breathe in the aroma of brewing coffee, listen to raindrops splashing on the window, bite slowly into that juicy peach, all of these things are products of God's common grace. After all, God could have given us K rations for our food, or made us eat straw like some animals.

Only when the optometrist tells us we are losing sight in an eye do we truly value our vision. Helen Keller, born deaf, mute, and blind, advised people to use their eyes as if tomorrow they would be blind. She recounted what she would do, if she had only three days to use her eyes. First, she would visit all the people who had befriended her and look lovingly at their faces. Then, after also gazing intently on a baby, she would walk slowly through the woods. The second day, after seeing the sun rise, she would tour museums and places of art and science and industry. That night she would watch the grace and beauty of a ballet. The last day she would again rise early to watch dawn break. Then she would visit schools and playgrounds before standing on a street corner to observe the ache and suffering of passing crowds. That night she would attend a comedy to observe the greatness of the human spirit which can laugh at its own foibles.

Though we might use the three days differently than Helen Keller, she reminds us that sight, along with the other senses, contributes richly to our happiness.

We have just scratched the surface of the common joys available to mankind. Joy comes at recovery from illness, at the reversal of an oppressive or ugly situation, at escape from accident, at triumph over tragedy. Leisure, sports, fun, holidays, horseback riding, winning a race, breaking a record, catching a big fish, a first plane ride, skiing, skating, boating, diving, swimming all have their ecstasies. In the book, *Happiness Is a Warm Puppy*, happiness is being able to reach door knobs, finding a pal at the door, a thumb and a blanket, smooth sidewalks when you're on roller skates, and three friends in a sandbox and no fighting.

Need for Cultivating Common Joys
The usual poker game was in progress on a morning commuter train running south along the Hudson River toward New York City. One of the players, happening to glance out the window, exclaimed in surprise, "Look, fellows, there's a river!"

Not only have common joys been missed because of obsession with trivia, but also because of a mistaken philosophy. This philosophy holds that common, sense-pleasing joys should be crucified because they are incompatible with high-grade sanctity. Rather we should awaken every morning in eager anticipation of the seemingly small, yet significant, blessings awaiting us that day. "This is the day which the Lord hath made; we will rejoice and be glad in it" (Ps. 118:24).

Common Joys Enhanced by the Gospel

Though common grace grants common joys to everyone, these common joys can be enhanced by special grace. For believers, common joys take on deeper meaning. When we have peace through Christ, common joys take on added zest through the work of the Holy Spirit.

For example, nature takes on new dimensions. Investigation of scientific laws becomes a process of thinking God's thoughts after Him. The wonders of the stars and of plant and animal life are seen as the handiwork of God. Before his conversion, Jonathan Edwards was unusually terrified of thunderstorms. But afterward, he would watch the play of lightning and listen to the majestic and awful voice of God's thunder. This led him "to sweet contemplations of my great and glorious God. While thus engaged, it always seemed natural to me to sing, or chant" (Russell T. Hitt, ed., *Heroic Colonial Christians*, Lippincott, 1966, p. 34).

When D.L. Moody came out of his rooming house the Sunday morning after his conversion, he thought the sun shone more brightly than ever before, and that the birds were singing to him.

Common joy also can be found in family life. Some non-Christian couples may *seem* happier than some Christian couples. But the potential for a happy Christian marriage far exceeds the potential for a happy non-Christian marriage. Marriage partners who are drawn toward Christ are drawn toward each other. Children are viewed as a loan from the Lord. The parents are responsible to Him for their upbringing. This stewardship concept intensifies the joys of parenthood.

But God wants us to be good stewards in other areas too. Our friendships are deepened when both persons in a relationship know the Lord. Each one cares for the other with a burden-bearing love that continues through eternity. Our possessions also take on new significance when acknowledged as a gift from God who owns everything. Even work becomes an extension of creation and a duty to be faithfully performed as to the Lord.

The Book of Ecclesiastes is universally quoted to show the vexation and vanity that comes with the common joys of life. Yet the ancient Hebrews read Ecclesiastes publicly on the happiest of days, the Feast of Tabernacles. They knew its final message was not futility and emptiness, but rather abiding joy in a spiritually renewed life.

Dr. A.J. Gordon, for many years a pastor in Boston, one day met a little boy in front of his church. The boy carried a rusty birdcage in which several small birds fluttered around and chirped sadly. He had trapped them in a field, and said he planned to feed them to an old cat at home. Dr. Gordon bought the cage and the birds for $2. Behind the church he opened the cage and watched the birds soar into the sky. Next Sunday Dr. Gordon took the empty cage into the pulpit and used the incident in his sermon. "That little boy said the birds could not sing very well. But when I released them from the cage, they went singing away into the blue. And it seems they were singing, 'Redeemed, Redeemed, Redeemed!'"

John Masefield wrote in *The Everlasting Mercy:*

O glory of the lighted mind,
How dead I'd been, how dumb, how blind.
The station brook, to my new eyes,
Was babbling out of paradise,
The waters rushing from the rain,
Were singing Christ has risen again.
I thought all earthly creatures knelt
From rapture of the joy I felt.

The unsaved can sing because of common joys. But how much better we sing after we have been redeemed. With the psalmist we say, "Bless the Lord, O my soul, and forget not all His benefits" (103:2).

5
Entrance to the Highway of Joy

In *Pilgrim's Progress*, John Bunyan described Pilgrim coming to a highway, fenced in on both sides by a wall called Salvation. Up this highway he ran, but with great difficulty because of the load on his back. After a while, burdened Pilgrim came to an elevation on which stood a cross, and below it, a sepulcher. Just as Pilgrim arrived at the cross, his burden fell off his back, and tumbled out of sight into the grave. He was relieved.

Then an angel announced, "Thy sins be forgiven thee." Another angel stripped him of his rags, and gave him new clothes. Then Pilgrim gave three leaps for joy, and went on his way singing.

The entrance to the highway of joy is the cross of Christ (followed by the empty tomb), through which we receive forgiveness for our sins. Among the greatest joys that can come to the human heart is the knowledge that God has forgiven all of our transgressions. Forgiven sinners exultantly join in the chorus, "Rolled away; every burden of my heart rolled away."

Man in his natural state is alienated from God. As violator of God's moral law, he suffers valid, guilt, which robs him of peace and joy. So man tries many ways to rid himself of his guilt.

Wrong Ways of Handling Guilt

Some people try to *neutralize* their wrongdoings. For every bad deed, they try to counter with a good deed. But a bank robber cannot successfully plead, "Yes, I robbed a bank, but think of the hundreds of banks I didn't rob." Or a thief will get nowhere, claiming, "I stole from the store so I could make a contribution to charity."

Some *rationalize* their sins. They blame their trespasses on bad genes, poor mates, their home lives, or on the whole world—"Everybody's doing it!"

Others *minimize* evil. They claim it has no reality, and is just an illusion of the mortal mind. Some *revise* their wrongs by renaming them. Temper becomes righteous indignation. Stinginess becomes economy. Stubbornness becomes firmness.

A committee member stormed out of a meeting because the chairman dared to disagree with him. He later insisted on making an open apology at a church business meeting. "In a recent committee meeting," he pompously began, "the chairman and I disagreed. During the discussion I became emphatic. Still the chairman did not see it my way, and I became more emphatic. Before the meeting was over, I became most emphatic. At that point I retired from the meeting. I would like to take this opportunity," he concluded, "to apologize to the chairman for becoming most emphatic."

Still others try to *anesthetize* their bad deeds. By a constant round of activity, or by using drugs or liquor, they try to drown out the condemning inner voice.

Right Way of Handling Guilt

None of these ways work. Guilt is real and must be handled, not accommodated or ignored. The proper way—the way of the Bible—is to recognize wrongdoing as sin in the sight of God, and ask Him to forgive us. God has provided a remedy in the Person of His Son, who came into this world to shed His blood for the remission of sins. He that covers his sins shall not prosper, but whoever confesses and forsakes evil shall have the blessing of God (Prov. 28:13).

The person who places his faith in the redeeming, finished work of Christ, receives the forgiveness of all his sins. When the impact of this momentous truth reaches his innermost being, he experiences great joy. For some, the delight will come suddenly; for others, it will come gradually. But in any case, the remedy is lasting, for it gets to the root of our problem. Forgiveness is not like a superficial massage that limbers up a few spots but fails to reach the real trouble. The deep therapy of divine forgiveness treats the root-cause of our alienation from God.

The Bible uses several figures of speech to describe what happens to the believers' sins. *Out of sight*. The prophet says to God, "Thou hast cast all my sins behind thy back" (Isa. 38:17). Though God doesn't literally have a back, the inspired writer pictured God in human form to teach us a wonderful truth. Our sins are out of God's sight, and out of ours too.

Another verse in Isaiah conveys the same truth. The Lord says, "I have blotted out, as a thick cloud, thy transgressions" (44:22). A dark cloud, hiding the morning sun, slowly evaporates until it entirely disappears from the sky, letting the sun shine forth. So our transgressions, which conceal the sunshine of God— when forgiven—vanish, thus letting the joy of the Lord saturate our life.

Out of reach. The psalmist declared that God has removed our transgressions from us "as far as the east is from the west" (103:12). Had the verse said, "As far as north is from the south," this distance could be measured, for Admiral Byrd visited both places. But east is east, and west is west—the two are entirely separated.

Micah wrote, "Thou wilt cast all their sins into the depths of the sea" (7:19). Ocean depths are black as ink, for no light can penetrate. One man said, "I've no desire to don a diving suit and go down to hunt them."

An enthusiastic Christian boy used to blurt out an occasional "Hallelujah" in school. Sent to the principal's office to explain his conduct, the boy was given a geography book to read for a few minutes. Suddenly, the principal heard a loud "Hallelujah." He asked how a geography text could excite the boy's religious enthusiasm. The student explained, "I just read that in one place scientists cannot find the ocean bottom. And my Bible tells me my sins have been buried in the bottom of the ocean. Hallelujah!"

Out of memory. God says, "I will remember their sin no more" (Jer. 31:34). God's memory differs from ours. We easily forget the things we should remember, and remember the things we would like to forget. But God recalls what He wishes to recall, and forgets what He wants to forget. He chooses to forget our iniquities.

The release of the live goat into the wilderness on the Day of Atonement, after the high priest had symbolically transferred the sins of the people to the animal's head, pictured the removal of believers' sins into the land of forgetfulness (Lev. 16:10).

Technically, God forgets nothing. In speaking of God's forgetfulness, we mean He doesn't hold it against us. No child of God needs to suffer gnawing guilt at his memory. Rather, the joys of sins forgiven and forgotten should grip his soul. If God forgets our iniquities, we should forget them too.

No joy can compare with the knowledge of sins forgiven. The psalmist exclaimed, "Blessed is he whose transgression is forgiven, whose sin is covered. Blessed is the man unto whom the Lord imputeth not iniquity" (32:1-2).

The 3,000 people who experienced the joy of forgiveness at Pentecost "did eat their meat with gladness" (Acts 2:46). Later, when the people of Samaria needed the good news of forgiveness, preached by Philip, "There was great joy in that city" (8:8). Likewise, when the Philippian jailer and his house believed on the Lord Jesus Christ, and were baptized, they rejoiced (16:34).

The Book of Romans has no mention of joy till the section on justification. After the opening chapters which declare man's sinfulness, Paul explains how a holy God can remain holy, and yet forgive unholy people—namely, by giving His Son as a sacrifice for our sins. By punishing sin in the Person of His Son, God maintains His righteousness, while He declares us righteous through Christ's substitutionary, redemptive death (Rom. 3:24-26).

Justification is the judicial act of God whereby because of Christ's shed blood, the sinner no longer faces the penalty of the Law. Rather, the sinner stands acquitted before God. Justification does not *make* a person righteous, but *declares* that he is righteous. This pronouncement brings delight. "Therefore being justified by faith, we have peace with God through our Lord Jesus Christ" (Rom. 5:1). (For an in-depth study of justification, refer to chap. 5 of Millard Erickson's *Salvation: God's Amazing Plan*, Victor, 1978, pp. 51-60.)

Long ago, France had a record book which listed the taxes due from each city, town, and village, with a page for each place. On the page assigned the little village of Domrémy was the amount to be paid to the government. But across the page, written in red ink, were the words, "Taxes remitted for Maid's sake." Because Joan of Arc was born there, a government grateful for her military triumph against the invading English had honored her native village with perpetual remission of taxes. Likewise, across the pages of believers' life histories are written the words, "Sins forgiven through the blood of Christ."

The day after his conversation, Dr. Alan Redpath, former pastor of Moody Church, Chicago, read Romans 8:1: "There is therefore now no condemnation to them which are in Christ Jesus." Overjoyed at the thought of no judgment for his sins, he underlined the words, "no condemnation" so heavily that he put a hole right through the following five of Paul's epistles.

Grace and *joy* are closely related. From the same root, the Greek words spell and sound similar: *charis* (grace) and *chara* (joy). Grace is that which causes joy. Joy comes through embracing the Gospel of grace. "We also joy in God through our Lord Jesus Christ, by whom we have now received the atonement" (Rom. 5:11).

The forgiveness of sins means that we will be in heaven some day. We exult not only on entering the state of blessedness, but we also "rejoice in hope of the glory of God" (Rom. 5:2). *Glory* refers to the ultimate future blessedness guaranteed us. The forgiven sinner should glow with unwavering optimism, for whatever happens along the way, the conclusion will be victorious.

Jesus told His disciples to rejoice because their names were written in heaven (Luke 10:20). Though we shall be judged for our works as believers, we shall never be sent to a lost eternity, for Christ has already suffered hell for us. Either death or Christ's return will dispatch us into His presence to be eternally with Him. Such assurance brings unspeakable joy, part of the comfort Jesus promised. He said, "Let not your heart be troubled," and then spoke of heavenly mansions He would prepare for believers (John 14:1-3).

A boy living in northern Idaho could never forget a timber buyer named Benham who stopped for a week in the boy's home. An outspoken atheist, Mr. Benham persuasively recited the main arguments of the skeptic, Robert G. Ingersoll. Irrevocably, Benham held that God did not exist; neither did heaven nor hell. To him, this life was all that mattered.

Twenty years later, the boy, now a successful businessman attending a convention in St. Paul, Minnesota, noticed a familiar-looking, gray-haired gentleman in the lobby. It was Mr. Benham who, remembering him as a boy, invited him to lunch. The businessman immediately noticed that the atheist had lost his poise. Now 71, Mr. Benham explained he had only months to live because of incurable anemia.

He then launched into an unforgettable story about an elderly lady who was dying in a hospital where he had gone for a checkup. Conscripted by a nurse, and then sent out by the dying woman to get three witnesses to a deathbed will, Mr. Benham was struck with the utter serenity of this woman, who faced the end with a smiling countenance.

The nurse rapidly wrote the whispered instructions of the stricken woman. When the three witnesses had signed the paper, the lady smiled, thanked them, and said, "And now I am ready to leave this pain-wracked body to meet my Maker, my husband, my father, my mother, and all my friends who have gone on before me. Won't that be wonderful?"

As Mr. Benham reached this point, tears started coming down his pale, wrinkled cheeks. "Look at me," he whispered hoarsely. "I've lain awake nights since I learned my days were numbered, staring at the ceiling with nothing to look forward to, except that my life would end in a handful of ashes. That's the difference between me, an atheist, and that lady. She, believing, faces her final days with a smile. I, an unbeliever, with every moment a nightmare, face nothing but a cold tomb." Then he added, "I would shove my hands into a bed of hot coals if, by so doing, I could secure a belief in a Supreme Being and an afterlife."

Paul revealed a major source of his joy when he wrote, "I know whom I have believed, and am persuaded that He is able to keep that which I have committed unto Him against that day (2 Tim. 1:12).

Once on the highway of joy, after entering by way of the cross and forgiveness, we find that the road leads to many other avenues of spiritual delight. Let's explore some of these thoroughfares.

6 Avenues to Spiritual Joys

A man on his way to work met a friend who greeted him, "Good morning." Grumpily, the friend replied, "What's so good about it?"

Another fellow carried a sign which read, "I made one mistake today. I got up."

Followers of Christ should not begin a day in poor spirits. For them, joy *should* be the norm. But joy does not come automatically. Even though a person may have entered the highway of joy through the gate of forgiveness, God does not guarantee constant spiritual rapture from the moment of conversion till the end of life. Though joy comes through a right relationship with Christ, it is maintained by obedience to His precepts. Jesus said, "If ye know these things, happy are ye if ye do them" (John 13:17).

Remember, joy does not come when we pursue it. But when we pursue our duty to Christ, joy will follow. Joy is not a goal, but a result of disciplined walking God's avenues of obedience. This principle holds in many areas of life. For example, the concert violinist does not go to the recital hall concentrating on happiness. But after a masterful performance, great gladness surges over him. Joy is the result of faithful practice.

The fruit grower must follow the procedures of good farming if he wants a healthy crop of oranges. He prunes his trees, sprays against insects, fertilizes and waters the soil; and when frost menaces, builds smudge-pots. Likewise, the fruit of joy, produced in us by the Holy Spirit, becomes more abundant after God prunes our lives with spiritual disciplines.

Let's look at some avenues which, if followed, will help us walk as jubilant kings instead of gloomy beggars. Perhaps the genuine joys could be called spiritual highs. In contrast to common joys, spiritual highs are experienced by believers only.

Meditation in the Word

Joyful (or blessed) is the man whose delight is in the law of the Lord (Ps. 1:1-3). The psalmist found the Scriptures to be the rejoicing of his heart (119:111).

Meditation in God's Word contributes to our spiritual strength, and in turn, spiritual strength makes for happiness. Paul urged believers to maintain healthy (sound) words, doctrine, and faith (2 Tim. 1:13; Titus 1:9, 13). A daily diet of spiritual food enables us to face the various crises of life. Our ways become more and more conformed to the majestic ideals of God.

For example, we learn that God cares for us, and esteems us of much greater value than the birds and flowers (Luke 12:6, 27-28). God never leaves, nor forsakes us. When trouble comes, we rest in the promise that, for those who love God, all things work together for good (Rom. 8:28). All of these truths promote joy.

To expect joy by mood instead of by mind is to build on a flimsy foundation. Yet often we run our churches with more emphasis on emotional response than on intellectual stimulation. The preacher is supposed to be an inspirator who helps worshipers *feel* devotional, rather than a teacher who instructs in Bible truths. Admittedly, we need both. But many adults prefer the worship hour to the Sunday school class.

The Old Testament emphasizes teaching. "Now these are the commandments, the statutes, and the judgments, which the Lord your God commanded to teach you, that ye might do them. . . . Hear, therefore, O Israel, and observe to do it; that it may be well with thee" (Deut. 6:1, 3). *That it may be well with thee* could be paraphrased "that you may be happy." Joy accompanies meditation and obedience.

Just as hunger or malnutrition makes us edgy and ready to flare up at minor irritations, so lack of biblical food leads to spiritual illness. If we don't devour the Word, we'll devour one another (Gal. 5:15).

On the other hand, scriptural saturation leads to joyful unity. If we let the Word of Christ dwell in us richly, we then can teach and admonish one another with psalms, hymns, and spiritual songs (Col. 3:16).

God's Word is an ever-flowing fountain of joy because of its numerous promises, its emphasis on eternal values, its purification of the mind, and its encouragements and corrections. It speaks of a wisdom this world knows nothing about, a peace the world cannot give, and a hope that looks beyond earthly horizons. No wonder Jeremiah wrote, "Thy words were found, and I did eat them; and Thy word was unto me the joy and rejoicing of mine heart" (15:16).

We may experience the deep-down joy of the disciples who, after talking with Jesus on the road to Emmaus, said to each other, "Did not our heart burn within us . . . while He opened to us the Scriptures?" (Luke 24:32)

Prayer

Before he became a missionary to Burma, Adoniram Judson wrote in his diary, "I have this day attained more than ever to what I suppose Christians mean by the enjoyment of God. I have had pleasant seasons at the throne of God" (Edward Judson, *The Life of Adoniram Judson,* American Baptist Publication Society, 1883, p. 14).

The psalmist testified of the joy of communion with God. "In Thy presence is fulness of joy; at Thy right hand there are pleasures for evermore" (16:11).

Answers to prayer rejoice the heart. Eleazar, commissioned by Abraham to find a wife for Isaac, not only found the *right* girl, but also a girl who was beautiful and helpful. Her fetching of water for Eleazar's camels was quite a chore, indicating a kind, generous, industrious, and a willing worker. Eleazar's joy brought adoration, "Blessed be the Lord God of my master Abraham, who hath not left destitute my master of His mercy and His truth" (Gen. 24:27).

We can see God work as He answers our prayers too. Jesus said to His disciples, "Hitherto have ye asked nothing in My name; ask, and ye shall receive, that your joy may be full" (John 16:24).

Worship
Corporate worship brings joy as we share with others in the adoration and praise of God. We say with David, "I was glad when they said unto me, 'Let us go into the house of the Lord'" (Ps. 122:1).

Contemplation of God's attributes and glorious works can lift us above the gloom of our limited perspectives. God is in control. He is never surprised by events that surprise us. Neither is He worried over world conditions. We trust in His ultimate victory. Realizing our lives are powerless and finite, we rest in Him who is Lord of all. His grace, mercy, and lovingkindness overwhelm us.

Fellowship
When its members are not on speaking terms with each other, a church becomes sterile and joyless. But where love prevails, fellowship brings felicity.

Paul found joy from his long-time fellowship with the Philippians, and when separated from them, he looked forward to seeing them again (Phil. 1:3-5, 26). Paul had a host of believer-friends, scattered in various places. He wrote to Timothy of his great desire "to see thee . . . that I may be filled with joy" (2 Tim. 1:4). The fellowship of like-minded disciples is joy-infusing.

Soul-Winning
The captain of a boat which made a daring rescue of 69 passengers from a plane downed in the North Atlantic said, "There is no greater happiness than in pul-

ling people out of the sea. You cannot get that kind of happiness making any amount of money!"

But greater joy comes from having a part in rescuing perishing souls from sin. James wrote, "He which converteth the sinner from the error of his way shall save a soul from death, and shall hide a multitude of sins" (5:20).

One March an old fur trapper in the north country was pushing his canoe through the loose ice. Then he heard something nearby. Calculating no human could be within 100 miles, he thought it must be a moose. He cocked his rifle in one hand, and pushed his canoe with the other. Carefully, he rounded the point and saw, not a moose, but a man wading in the ice water. His hands and feet were bare and his clothes were almost torn off. He was wasted to a skeleton.

The hunter got the man into his canoe, took him to his quarters, gave him hot food and tea, and nursed him like an infant. With great difficulty the hunter elicited the name of the place where the man lived. After a week's difficult travel, around falls and over rough terrain, keeping careful watch lest in his demented state the man escape into the forest, the hunter took him home.

The whole town was in deep excitement. More than 100 men were scattered in woods and mountains looking for him. The townspeople had agreed that if he were found, the bells should be immediately rung and guns should be fired. As soon as the hunter landed, the man's friends rushed to greet him. The bells pealed loudly, and the guns fired, their reports echoing again and again in the forest till every seeker knew that the lost was found.

The hunter had to tell his story again and again. People were overjoyed, for the man came from one of the best families. Later, the man's memory came back in a full recovery. The townsfolk feasted with the hunter and loaded his canoe with provisions and clothing.

Joy spreads in so many directions when a lost person is converted: to the new believer, to his loved ones who have prayed so earnestly, to those who have had a share in winning him—and even to heaven, for the angels rejoice over one sinner that repents (Luke 15:1-10).

Dr. John Broadus, seminary professor who wrote a classic text on homiletics, as a young man won his first convert to Christ. Thereafter, whenever this friend passed him on the street, he would invariably touch his hat and say, "Thank you, John, thank you."

The psalmist stated that "he that goeth forth and weepeth, bearing precious seed, shall doubtless come again with rejoicing, bringing his sheaves with him" (Ps. 126:6). Paul called his converts his joy and crown of rejoicing (Phil. 4:1; 1 Thes. 2:19-20). Corrie ten Boom often quoted this little verse,

> When I enter the beautiful city
> And the saints in glory draw near,
> I want someone to greet me, and tell me,
> It was you who invited me here.

On his way to Jerusalem for the first church council, Paul carried reports of numerous Gentile conversions. This brought joy to the brethren (Acts 15:3). But spiritual growth is also important. The growth of fellow-believers always pleased Paul, such as the steadfastness of the Colossians, and the faith of the

Thessalonians believers (Col. 2:5; 1 Thes. 3:9).

Persecution and Tribulation

Obviously, persecution is not an avenue we would deliberately choose to walk, but paradoxically, this *is* a highway that produces joy. Jesus said that when men revile or persecute us, we should rejoice and be exceedingly glad (Matt. 5:11-12).

After a beating, the apostles rejoiced that they were counted worthy to suffer shame for Jesus' name (Acts 5:41). Even our Saviour was not exempt from suffering. For the joy set before Him, Jesus endured the cross (Heb. 12:2).

Peter told believers that when fiery trials came their way, they were to rejoice, because they were partakers of Christ's sufferings" (1 Peter 4:12-13). Thus, we are to "count it all joy" when we fall into various testings, for these trials will help us develop patience (James 1:2-4).

Other Avenues

We have not exhausted the many avenues, which when traveled, are accompanied by joy. For example, fair treatment of others brings the reward of happiness (Ps. 106:3; Prov. 21:15). Also, doing good to others brings joy. Who hasn't experienced the warm glow that comes from performing a kind deed without any thought of recognition. Helen Steiner Rice wrote:

> For in making others happy
> We will be happy, too.
> For the happiness you give away
> Returns to "shine on you."
>
> *Someone Cares*, Revell, 1972, p. 39.

In general, obedience is the highway that produces divine joy. Pioneer missionary Ann Judson wrote in her diary, "Exposed to robbers by night and invaders by day, yet we both unite in saying we never were happier, never more contented in any situation, than the present. We feel that this is the post to which God hath appointed us; that we are in the path of duty" (Ethel Daniels Hubbard, *Ann of Ava,* Friendship Press, 1913, p. 70).

Through moment by moment committal to Christ, we are filled with His Spirit. In this continuous, ongoing process, He does not leave a surrendered vessel empty. Rather, His Spirit gives us joy.

Daily, Jesus found delight in doing His Father's bidding. He testified, "My meat is to do the will of Him that sent Me" (John 4:34). From experience He could say, "Blessed are they that hear the Word of God, and keep it" (Luke 11:28).

At the very onset of His ministry, Christ spoke of happiness. In 10 sentences, known as the Beatitudes, He charted the way to happiness. He emphasized, not our success or interests, but His kingdom. Poverty of spirit, and mourning over this bankruptcy, bring the wealth and comfort of the kingdom. Extending mercy toward others, purity of heart, irenic spirit, and suffering for righteousness' sake, all are escorted by blessedness.

Joy does not come unconditionally in the Christian's life, but as a result of a disciplined walk down designated highways. To maintain a high quality of joy, we prune our lives by spiritual practices. We enrich our inner self through the Word and soul-winning. To resist carnal blight, we pray and submit to God. The warmth of worship and fellowship is also ours—but we must not forget to fight the chilling frost of apathy.

The winning athlete finds joy at the end of the race, as he stands on the victor's stand to receive his prize. So, the faithful child of God will one day receive the crown of victory from the hand of the Judge and hear Him say, "Well done . . . enter thou into the joy of the Lord" (Matt. 25:21).

7 The Joy of Giving

A cartoon showed a smiling man waving dollar bills around, before tossing them into a big bag. The caption read, "In fund raising, happiness is counting the money!" But Christianity reverses this remark to read, "Happiness is contributing the money!" Jesus said, "It is more blessed to give than to receive" (Acts 20:35).

To receive is satisfying. A young man, given his first paycheck on his first job, went to the bank to cash it. "Endorse it, and I'll be glad to give you the money," said the teller. The youth, who had never before cashed a check, wrote on the back of it, "I heartily endorse the sentiments expressed herein." Though people do laugh all the way to the bank with their receipts, a significant lack is found in those who are always on the receiving or grasping end.

Many have never learned the truth that more joy comes from giving than from receiving. A well-known underworld figure walked into a 1957 Billy Graham crusade meeting in Madison Square Garden. At offering time, the henchmen, who flanked the mobster on both sides, looked toward him to see what they ought to do. He turned to them, "Men, this is on me." Pulling a roll of $100 bills from his wallet, he went through the thick wad till he came to a $1 bill, which he dropped on the plate. He had no concept of the joy of giving.

But even Christians can give without experiencing joy, like the lady visiting a mission chapel who dropped a $10 bill on the offering plate by mistake, and after the service tried to exchange it for the $1 bill she meant to give.

Or like the church that was $25,000 in debt. When the treasurer moved away, the manager of the local grain elevator agreed to take over the job under two conditions. First, no treasurer's report would be required during the first year. Second, no one would ask him any questions.

At the end of the year, he gave a glowing report. The church's debt of $25,000 had been fully met; the missions' budget had been doubled; the minister's salary had been raised considerably; and the treasury showed a balance of $12,000.

He explained to the surprised congregation, "Most of you sell your grain at my elevator. As you did business with me, I withheld 10 percent of your income on your behalf and gave it to the church in your name. At the end of the calendar year, I'll give you a receipt for income tax purposes. But you've never missed the money. Not once have you questioned me about the amount I gave you for your grain. Next year I won't do this. You'll be on your own." Because they gave unknowingly, these church members missed the *joy* of giving.

When the Israelites in the wilderness were asked to offer materials for the building of the tabernacle, "they came, every one whose heart stirred him up, and every one whom his spirit made willing, and they brought the Lord's offering to the work of the tabernacle" (Ex. 35:21). These donors experienced the joy of giving.

To help build Solomon's temple four centuries later, the Israelites once again contributed generously and eagerly. "Then the people rejoiced, for that they offered willingly, because with perfect heart they offered willingly to the Lord; and David the king also rejoiced with great joy" (1 Chron. 29:9). Everyone gave to God, even the king.

Over a century later, when the temple needed major repairs, King Joash placed a chest at the gate of the Lord's house. An announcement was made "to bring in to the Lord the collection that Moses the servant of God laid upon Israel in the wilderness" (2 Chron. 24:9). Again, the delight of giving was experienced, as "all the princes and all the people rejoiced, and brought in, and cast into the chest, until they had made an end" (v. 10). The Israelites knew what giving to God really meant.

When a person approaches the act of giving with the right attitude, he will be doubly joyful—his cheerful heart will be rewarded with the joy from giving.

But why is it more blessed to give than to receive? Why does giving yield joy?

Our Giving Helps Others

A poor young man worked hard to buy an expensive gift for his mother. Asked how he could afford it, he simply replied, "It was worth it all to see my mother smile."

Joy has been likened to a bottle of perfume on a shelf inside you. When you spill some on others, you cannot help spilling some on yourself.

The Christians at Philippi understood this lesson. Apparently, they helped Paul financially more than any other group of believers. Paul wrote them, " . . . no church communicated with me as concerning giving and receiving, but ye only" (Phil. 4:15). Thus they became stockholders in Paul's ministry.

When Paul wrote the letter to the Philippians, he was a prisoner in his own rented house. He needed money for rent, for food, and perhaps for medicine and clothes. Their gifts buoyed him up, kept him going, and brought salvation to the heathen. For even in Paul's detention, he carried on an effective ministry, witnessing to the runaway slave, Onesimus, and to anyone else who came by. Learning how their money had helped Paul must have brought elation to the Philippians.

One Monday morning a wealthy businessman met his minister on the street. "Pastor, you gave a magnificent sermon yesterday morning about heaven. But you never did tell us where heaven is."

"I'm glad you said that," replied the pastor. "Do you see that little cottage on top of the hill? I've just come from there. An old widow lives there and she is sick with a high fever. She's terribly poor. It's winter. But there's not a piece of wood nor a lump of coal in the shed. And she has no food in her cupboard. If you'll go down town and order fuel and food for her, then later take your wife and make a visit there, you might get an answer to your question."

The man, though rich, was not happy. He accepted the pastor's challenge, ordered fuel and food, then took his wife to make a visit. His heart was moved by the privation of that home. Before he left, he knelt by a chair, lifting his heart in supplication for the needs of that widow. He also included a request for help to overcome his own spiritual lack.

The next day he met his pastor again. It was the pastor's turn to have a mischievous twinkle in his eye. "Well, have you found out yet where heaven is?"

In a voice full of emotion, the wealthy parishioner replied, "Oh yes, Pastor, I now know where heaven is. I spent 30 minutes in heaven yesterday afternoon in that home where you sent my wife and me."

According to the Book of Proverbs, happiness comes to the man who helps the poor. When we bring material or spiritual aid to others, leading them to see some new truth, and strengthening them in the faith, this brings genuine joy. As John Greenleaf Whittier put it:

> Somehow, not only for Christmas
> But all the long year through,
> The joy that you give to others
> Is the joy that comes back to you.

Part of God's Nature

God is a giving God. Every good and perfect gift comes from His hand. He makes the sun to shine, and the rain to fall, on both the just and unjust. Daily, He loads us with benefits.

Moreover, God is generous in His giving. He lavishes His gifts on us abundantly. Though every snowflake is different, its individual beauty goes unnoticed by the unaided eye. A profusion of wilderness flowers wastes their "sweetness on the desert air." With great liberality the Giver showers His gifts on us.

A boy was hired to pick cherries with the stipulation that he couldn't eat a single one—a rather rigorous rule for a hungry, healthy boy. At the end of the day, the farmer commented, "Since you've kept your word, you may have a handful of cherries for yourself." But the boy didn't move toward the pail of cherries. "Didn't you hear?" asked the farmer. "Yes," replied the boy, "but please, Sir, I would rather you gave them to me." He knew the farmer's hand was much larger than his. In the same way, God exults in supplying us with blessings from a big, bountiful hand.

All members of the Trinity are involved in giving. The Father so loved the world that He gave His Son. Not only did He not spare His only Son, but with Him He also freely gives us a host of spiritual benefits (Rom. 8:32).

God's giving is not limited to the Father. The Son willingly gave Himself and laid down His life for us. No man took his life from Him, for He volunteered it. Likewise, the Holy Spirit has given gifts to the church to help it mature into the image of Christ.

Believers are exhorted again and again to reflect the giving image of the divine family into which they have been born anew by giving of themselves, their time, their gifts, their talents, their money, their all.

Paul wrote, "I beseech you . . . that you present your bodies a living sacrifice" (Rom. 12:1).

A wealthy Christian layman, challenged to make a donation to a worthy missionary cause, curtly declined, complaining, "As far as I can see, this business of Christianity is just one continuous give, give, give." Came the answer, "I wish to thank you for the best definition of the Christian life that I have ever heard."

In contrast to this reluctant giver, countless Christians following the example of the living and giving God, have experienced the thrill of sacrificial giving.

Let's not forget that the beatitude on giving came from Jesus. The best known beatitudes are from the Sermon on the Mount. But this beatitude on giving was not included in that list. Grippingly simple, yet profound, this saying was part of Paul's farewell address to the Ephesian elders. Encouraging them to support the weak, he reminded them of the words of the Lord Jesus, "how He said, 'It is more blessed to give than to receive'" (Acts 20:35).

Giving Yields Joy

The delight of giving is another common joy which non-Christians may experience. But, like other common joys, giving for the Christian brings delight that unbelievers cannot experience.

Though giving lays up treasures for future heavenly bliss, the act of unselfish sharing brings immediate joy. A sense of satisfaction accompanies a genuine act of sharing: the parents who give to a helpless child; the friend who helps another friend; the neighbor who gives to the needy; the philanthropist who sacrificially denies self to promote a worthy cause.

Mental health expert Dr. William Menninger said, "No matter what your age or job in life, you are more mature if you have found a 'cause' in which to invest your time and money for some social good. Through it you can achieve an outstanding characteristic of emotional maturity—the ability to find satisfaction in giving" (*Think*, September-October 1966, p. 21).

Sir Launfal's vision contains these words:

Not what we give, but what we share,

For the gift without the giver is bare;

Who giveth himself with his alms, feeds three,

Himself, his hungering neighbor and me.

James R. Lowell, *The Vision of Sir Launfal*, Allyn and Bacon, 1900, p. 12)

Christian giving should be regular, proportional, sincere, willing, cheerful, expectant, and generous. Though a motto says, "Give till it hurts," genuine giving should not make us hurt, but should make us happy.

We are responsible to give intelligently, not indiscriminately. A teenage girl stood in front of a department store rattling a can and crying, "Give something for the orphans." Coins tinkled plentifully into the can despite the clear printing on its front, which declared the scheme a fraud: "Give! Three-headed Orphans of Claustrophobia. This is a FAKE." The girl had been positioned on the street to see how gullible people were. In four cities where the test was made, only 4 persons out of the 264 who stopped, discovered the fraud. And about 60 percent gave something (David Dressler, "Scoundrels and Scalawags," *Readers's Digest*, 1968).

Many years ago, in a Pennsylvania town, several members of a church agreed with the pastor to stop giving to foreign missions. But other members favored overseas evangelism. The division became so marked that the non-missionary-minded members locked the other members out of the meeting house. The pastor declared that he would remain at the church as long as he had one person in the congregation. And that he did, for the congregation dwindled to one. When that member died, the church became dilapidated, and was converted into a saloon.

When this story appeared in print, all that remained as a memorial to those who had voted against giving to missions, was a cemetery located in the spot where the church had once stood. But those locked out because of their missionary zeal built a small structure which flourished so much that they had to build a bigger building. Today they give several thousands of dollars to missions annually.

Jesus said, "Give, and it shall be given unto you; good measure, pressed down, and shaken together, and running over" (Luke 6:38). And give with joy, like the 10-year-old girl who said, "Daddy, I seem to have the most joy when I bring joy to you."

The Holy Land has two good-sized seas. Alive, sparkling, and lovely, the Sea of Galilee is used today by fishermen, as it was in the days of Jesus. The other is the Dead Sea, in which nothing lives, for it's polluted, and saturated with chemicals. Why is one living, and the other dead? Because the Dead Sea gives nothing out. No river flows from it, though the Jordan River flows into it. In contrast, the Sea of Galilee not only has the Jordan flowing into it, but also flowing out. The Sea of Galilee is alive because it gives.

If we make a regular practice of giving of ourselves to others, we cannot help but be the recipients of genuine joy.

8
The Oil of Gladness

Life can become a bore and a chore, a wearying business like wading through thick honey. Frustrations and disappointments accumulate like dust, building up monotony and moodiness. But God has provided a lubrication to counteract the erosions of daily living. Joy is the oil that lessens the wear and tear of mundane frictions. A continual flow of the oil of gladness gives zest to all our activities.

Christians are not meant to live dismally nor drearily. Dr. A.B. Simpson pointed out that God's Old Testament people enjoyed a constant succession of feasts which the whole nation was required to observe. Three times a year the nation had a mammoth religious holiday. These holidays kept the people from becoming melancholy.

After the return from exile, the Israelites came to observe the Feast of Tabernacles. But they were sad because of the desolation of Zion. Nehemiah told them not to mourn, "for the joy of the Lord is your strength" (8:10). Joy gives strength to do God's will.

Significantly, the doing of God's will and the feeling of genuine joy act reciprocally to set up a perpetual chain of action. Doing God's will is followed by joy. Then joy, in turn, provides strength to obey God's commands. This obedience yields more joy, which again provides the impetus for more submission to the divine will. This continuous, recurring cycle of joy—obedience—joy—obedience makes for a high level of Christian walk.

Let's explore some areas in which joy makes it easier to pursue the Christian path.

Strength in Worship

An editor in *Decision* magazine wrote, "Try to be a good churchman without the joy of Christ: the sermon becomes an endurance contest, the hymns an exercise in tedium, the offering an ordeal by extraction" (July 1964).

But the joy of the Lord can make worship a pleasure. Joy makes us praise. The triumphant Red Sea crossing brought forth the song of Moses. The healed demoniac, the woman bent with infirmity for 18 years, and the cleansed leper all broke forth in grateful praise to God.

A taxi driver, whose stand was located outside a church, was asked by a stranger one Sunday morning what time the service ended. He replied, "Fairly soon now. They usually have three big noises, a long pause of about half an hour, then a fourth big noise. So far they've only had three noises." It is true that the redeemed of the Lord can more easily make a loud noise when they are full of joy.

Often, large congregations in expansive sanctuaries sing poorly, while small groups in store-front structures nearly lift the roof off with their enthusiastic singing. The store-front worshipers are inspired by their deep-down joy.

A children's chorus goes like this:

> When my cup runneth over with joy,
> It is easy to sing all the day.

But when our cup is empty and dry, then it's easy to sit down and cry. Without joy, we revert to grumbling.

Joy helps us pray. The command to rejoice immediately precedes the command to pray. "Rejoice evermore. Pray without ceasing" (1 Thes. 5:16-17). Without inner melody, prayer becomes a metallic noise.

Strength in Woe

Sir Isaac Newton once lost all the calculations of 25 years when his valuable papers were burned up because of a little dog's playfulness. Newton's sunny serenity helped him react mildly, "Poor thing! You little know the mischief you've done!"

Not only in disappointments but also in sickness and suffering can the joy of the Lord sustain us. A new pastor was asked to visit a lady who had been an invalid for 16 years. She was nearly blind. Her arms and legs were twisted. She was never without pain. Yet she asked the pastor if he would join her in a song. She requested, "There Is Sunshine in My Soul Today."

George Matheson, a hymn writer, lost his sight as a youth and spent 30 years in darkness. The source of his spiritual strength is suggested in the third stanza of his well-known hymn, "O Love That Wilt Not Let Me Go."

O joy that seekest me through pain,
I cannot close my heart to thee;
I trace the rainbow through the rain,
And feel the promise is not vain
That morn shall tearless be.

Fanny Crosby, blind from six weeks old, wrote the following at the age of eight:

O what a happy soul am I!
Although I cannot see.
I am resolved that in this world
Contented I will be;
How many blessings I enjoy
That other people don't!
To weep and sigh because I'm blind
I cannot, and I won't.

Before she died, in her 95th year, she had composed over 3,000 hymns, including some of our best known today.

The joy of the Lord always counts on the great Restorer and Recompenser to provide something better, if not now, then in the hereafter.

Someone asks, "Can I rejoice when my body is wracked with pain, and my mind distracted with care?" The oil of gladness can give strength to bear the pain and pressure. With their beaten backs bleeding and their feet positioned in stocks, Paul and Silas strengthened themselves by singing praises in the dungeon (Acts 16:25). Songs in the night bring light during darkness (Job 35:10).

When Paul wrote his letter to the Philippians, he

commanded them to rejoice—even though he was in prison and chained to a guard 24 hours a day. Facing the ordeal of a trial and possible death, he was still joyful.

The night before His crucifixion, Jesus spoke of His own joy, which doubtless gave Him strength to sing a hymn in the face of His coming agony (John 15:11; Matt. 26:30).

Joy was also evident on the face of the first martyr. Stephen's face shone angelically as he made his defense against the Sanhedrin (Acts 6:15). Inward joy enabled him not only to stand the stoning, but also to pray for his tormentors.

The day before John Huss was burned at the stake, he wrote, "I write this in prison and in chains, expecting tomorrow to receive sentence of death, full of hope in God that I shall not swerve from the truth. I will this day joyfully die."

A tract titled, "Seven Men Went Singing into Heaven," told how seven prisoners behind the iron curtain, at their request, faced the firing squad with faces uncovered. Then, with hands raised to heaven, they heartily sang, "Safe in the Arms of Jesus" (*Good News Tract of the Month*, no. 40, Good News Publishers).

Is it possible to rejoice when death snatches a loved one, making us "long for the touch of a vanished hand, and the sound of a voice that is still"? Of course, happiness flees, but midst the heartache, joy can be our strength. Natural sorrow can be attended by genuine joy which empowers us to sorrow differently from those who have no hope. Paradoxically, as in Paul's experience, we can be sorrowful, yet rejoicing.

Weeping may endure for a night, but joy comes in the morning (Ps. 30:5).

A Christian man, when asked the source of his radiance, told how he and his wife had longed for 10 years to have a child. Finally, their baby daughter was born. She brought much delight, especially since she would be their only child. Her sunny disposition earned her the nickname "Smiles."

But when she was 10, she suddenly became ill and died. Said the man, "I thought our world had ended. I walked the streets to control my feelings. Finally, I entered the room where the child lay in her coffin. Kneeling, I prayed, 'O Lord, if you will grant me the strength, I will go through life smiling for both of us.'" His smiling joy enabled him not only to live above the dark night of sorrow, but also to inspire hundreds of others.

Strength in Work, Warfare, and Witness

Although love is mentioned prior to joy in the list of the fruit of the Spirit, Jesus put joy before love in His discourse the night before He died. "These things have I spoken unto you, that My joy might remain in you and that your joy might be full. This is My commandment, that ye love one another" (John 15:11-12). Joy helps us to exhibit the rest of the fruit by being less irritable, less envious, less discourteous, more patient, more gentle, more kind, more humble, more self-controlled, more loving.

Melancholy paralyzes Christian work. When the Israelites lost their joy not long after the victorious Red Sea crossing, they yearned to return to Egypt. But joy is an energizing additive, putting us in the mood for service. How much easier to do our tasks when our hearts are light. John Bunyan carved a flute from the leg of a stool, almost the only piece of furniture in his jail cell. The resultant music encouraged him during his 12year imprisonment, helping to inspire the writing of his immortal allegory, *Pilgrim's Progress*.

When Judah was imperiled by an invading enemy, singers were appointed to join the defending army. When the Levites began to praise the Lord with loud voices in the valley of Berachah, the enemy was defeated (2 Chron. 20:21-26).

Music has stirred countless armies to battle courageously. Similarly, the joy of the Lord spurs us on in the war against the enemy of our souls. John Wesley wrote in his journal, "I do not remember to have felt lowness of spirit for one quarter hour. I see God sitting upon His throne and ruling all things well." Wesley's joy probably contributed to his many decades of continuous, unabated devotion to Christ's service.

Joy is an ingredient that helps bring real motivation, which is so missing in Christian circles today. When we've lost our song, we've lost our strength. Dr. Paul Rees, minister at large for World Vision, said, "We are not so much overworked as we are undermotivated." Joy makes us more readily take that Sunday School class, visit that shut-in, help in the nursing-home program, attend prayer meetings, minister in the inner city, or adopt an unwanted baby.

Strength in Worry

A magazine column titled, "Be Happier, Stay Healthier" reported on tests made at the Johns Hopkins School of Medicine in Baltimore. Psychological evaluations and personality tests given to a sizable group of healthy people revealed a correlation between temperament and rate of recovery from illness. Those with happier dispositions recovered from the flu in anywhere from three days to two weeks; the more pessimistic took three or more weeks.

Depression can trigger a staggering number of physical complaints like headaches, backaches, stomach troubles, and heart palpitations. A conservative estimate showed that at least 50 percent of those visiting doctors' offices with physical complaints were there because they were basically unhappy. Fatigue makes many dose themselves with tonics, vitamins, and pep pills (Lawrence Galton, "The Hidden Disease," *Pageant,* October 1957). But the real cure is the biblical merry heart that "doeth good like a medicine" (Prov. 17:22).

Today in America we have more 100-year-olds than ever before—around 9,000 according to the Social Security Administration, with numbers increasing annually. What is their secret? Though several factors contribute, the key characteristic shared by most centenarians is a cheerful disposition. Joy somehow lubricates the biological machinery to keep it running longer (Carol Blake, "Happiness—the Best Preventative Medicine," *Reader's Digest,* February 1976, pp. 130-132).

Joy is therapeutic and health-giving. A proverb says, "A man of gladness seldom falls into madness."

Strength to Prevent Whining

How easy it is to complain! The Israelites repeatedly

filled God's ear with grumblings about diet, water, and leadership. Had they kept the song of Moses, they would never have bemoaned the lack of water and food.

David experienced many occasions when whining could have been his natural reaction. Once when the wives and children of his followers were carried away into captivity, David could easily have been paralyzed by depression. Instead, he "encouraged himself in the Lord" (1 Sam. 30:6). So often when things were stacked against him, did he praise, rejoice, and take courage, banishing the blues. He knew that joy and complaining didn't mix.

Paul knew that if he could get those two ladies, Euodias and Syntyche, to sing together, their differences would soon be resolved. So in the same breath that he told them to be of the same mind in the Lord, he also ordered them to "rejoice in the Lord" (Phil. 4:3-4).

A joyful church will not be a murmuring nor a squabbling people. If we are rejoicing, we cannot be grumpy. Singing dispels sighing. The believers should be like tea kettles, which, when the pressure is on, don't whine but whistle.

Strength for Winsomeness

If a professing believer shows no outward joy, he shouldn't be surprised that people don't crave his spiritual "secret." But if anointed with the oil of gladness, as was Christ, he can become a joyful rebuttal of Nietzche's criticism: "I would believe in their salvation if they looked a little more like people who have been saved."

Paul's buoyancy in the face of violent storm and 14 sunless days gave him moral ascendency in a hopeless situation. "Be of good cheer," he told the others on board (Acts 27:22-25, 35-37).

A church filled with joyless Christians is a hindrance to spiritual revival. Hudson Taylor remarked, "Too often a long face suggests that people had better take their fill of happiness just before they leave it behind by becoming a Christian."

Chicago's Moody Church was packed to its 4,000 capacity for an anniversary service. The onetime chaplain-in-chief of British forces, Bishop Taylor-Smith, was the scheduled speaker. When the bishop came down with laryngitis, he was reluctant to speak, but the pastor insisted. The folks in the rear could not hear. Their politeness, plus the significance of the occasion, kept them from walking out. But at the end of the service, a man made his way to the bishop. "Sir, I could not escape the joy on your face. If to believe the Gospel means the coming of such a glow as I saw on your face, I want to confess Christ as my Saviour" (Paul S. Rees, *World Vision*, June 1964).

A joyful disposition may surpass a ton of logic, rhetoric, and apologetics. A scholarly minister once gave a series of sermons on the evidences of Christianity—for the special purpose of convincing a wealthy skeptic. The skeptic attended the lectures and became a Christian.

The minister later asked him which of the lectures had made him decide. "My dear sir," replied the former skeptic, "I don't even remember your lectures. I was converted by the testimony of that dear old lady who stood on the church steps before every service. With her face as bright as heaven she would say, 'My blessed Jesus! My blessed Jesus!' And turning to me, she would ask, 'Do you love my blessed Jesus?' That, sir, was my evidence of Christianity!"

Dr. R. Nelson Bell, distinguished missionary to China, declared, "In a world of growing tensions, nothing in a Christian's life does more to commend his faith to others than a serenity and joy independent of circumstances."

A reporter who visited the campus of Gordon College in Wenham, Mass. recently wrote in the *Beverly Times* that at this college, "Religion is a serious matter. And optimism and cheeriness seem to dominate the spirit of the Christian campus, leaving visitors with the feeling students and faculty know something they don't" (Richard Gross, president of Gordon College, to his constituency, 20 October 1978, Gordon College, Wenham, Mass.).

Paul Rader wrote, "When God chooses a man, He puts holy laughter into his life. Laughter, after all, is the surplus of life; it is a bubbling over of the emotions, a kind of spasm of exuberance; a delight of the human heart. . . . The joy of the Lord is our strength. It is the oil of His presence that makes holy laughter in the life—the ability to laugh at calamity, to laugh at death, to laugh at the victory which the devil thought he had won" (*Decision* magazine).

Religious melancholia turns people off, but contagious joy tells people that we have been with Jesus.

9 Serendipity

The word *serendipity* was coined by Horace Walpole in 1754 from the Persian fairy tale, *The Three Princes of Serendip* (sometimes spelled Serendib), another name for Ceylon. According to the legend, the king wanted his three sons to learn from experience what life was all about. So he sent them out, not as princes, but disguised as ordinary men. Traveling through the realm, they learned many things. But what impressed them most were the things they learned by accident. These extra pleasant, unexpected things were called *serendipities*.

Serendipity means making happy, unexpected discoveries, either by sagacity or by accident. It's the gift of finding valuable or agreeable things when not seeking them. The joy of serendipity usually involves the concepts of suddenness, surprise, and intensity, related to some definite event.

Would not the annunciations about their future

sons to Zacharias and Elizabeth, and Joseph and Mary be movingly pleasant experiences? Would not the visits of the shepherds the night of Jesus' birth, and later the worship by the Magi, joyfully surprise Joseph and Mary, as would the sudden outbursts of praise to their newborn babe in the temple by Simeon and Anna?

Would not the feeding of the 5,000, the walking on the water, the stilling of the stormy Sea of Galilee, and in fact, all of Jesus' miracles, qualify as serendipities for the disciples?

God has many unexpected delights for His children. "Eye hath not seen, nor ear heard, neither have entered into the heart of man, the things which God hath prepared for them that love Him" (1 Cor. 2:9). Often the Spirit suddenly reveals previously hidden nuggets of truth, as we read and study the Scriptures. A favorite expression of noted Bible teacher Dr. Wilbur M. Smith, repeated scores of times in the classroom and from the pulpit, and always with vigorous enthusiasm, was, "I never saw that truth before!"

Here are some areas of serendipities.

Common Blessings

An article, titled "Overtaken by Joy," described several overwhelming experiences with nature. A tourist in Nova Scotia told how, after a torrential downpour, the rain suddenly stopped as though a heavenly faucet had been turned off. Then a thin radiance, like a spray of gold, shone out from the clouds, catching the tops of trees and blades of grass with tremulous drops. A rainbow arched the sky, reaching on one side right into a nearby pond. The tourist, filled with awesome joy, found that he could hardly speak (Ardith Whitman, *Reader's Digest,* April 1965).

Psychologists tell us that many average, healthy individuals report similar experiences of deep delight. One man, swimming alone, and cavorting fish-like with almost insane delight, was so moved that he shouted over and over with sheer joy.

Almost any common event can trigger such joy: moonlight on fresh snow, a sudden garden of roses, a moment in marriage when hands touch automatically in the realization that the other feels as you feel. Perhaps what is needed is a child's spontaneous wonder of discovery.

Speedy restoration of health can stimulate a sense of joy. Think of the man born blind, washing his eyes in the pool of Siloam, then immediately seeing! Or imagine the man lame from birth, 40 years a cripple, suddenly being able to walk! No wonder he leaped and danced.

Even more striking is the example of the widow from Nain on her way to bury her only son. She saw Jesus take her boy by the hand and raise him up. Mary and Martha, after four days of grieving over their dead brother Lazarus, saw him emerge from the grave bound with graveclothes, then released to walk unhindered.

Answers to Prayer
Often while praying for something, the answer comes almost before the prayer is finished, a fulfillment of the Lord's promise: "And it shall come to pass that before they call, I will answer; and while they are yet speaking, I will hear" (Isa. 65:24).

New Testament believers met all night to pray for imprisoned Peter, who was scheduled for execution the next morning. When the Lord miraculously released him, the believers were astonished (Acts 12:13-16).

Our reaction to answered prayer is often similar to that of those early believers. When his plant closed down on Long Island, an electronic engineer was unable to find work. Down to their last can of chicken noodle soup, the family bowed their heads and prayed the Lord's Prayer.

The father, who loved to eat bread, was bothered that he and his family had none. With great deliberation they uttered, "Give us this day our daily bread." Just then came a persistent knocking at the back door. They hurried through the rest of the prayer, then the wife answered the door.

The father heard a neighbor's voice say, "Can you use any bread? My brother is a route man for one of the big companies. They've been having an advertising campaign in which they distribute little sample loaves of bread. He was given more than he needed for his stores. He has four cases left. He can't bring the cases back because the bread has got to be fresh each day. I've taken two cases and can't fit anymore in my house. Can you use the other two?"

The husband and wife were astonished at the immediacy and sufficiency of the answer. After the caller left, they praised and thanked God for bread in the breadbox, bread in the refrigerator, bread in the freezer, and bread on the table. Shortly thereafter, the husband was able to find work, but they always thanked God for their serendipitous experience.

Discoveries of Unknown Influence and Usefulness

Uncle Win Ruelke, well-known New York metropolitan children's worker, spoke in chapel at Northeastern Bible College in New Jersey. After the service, a student asked him if he had ever conducted a television series for boys and girls. Ruelke then learned that his program had been responsible for the conversion of that student about eight years before. Now the student was training for the ministry—an unexpected, delightful discovery for Ruelke.

A missionary appointee was giving a testimony in a church service. The pastor had never met the appointee, who was visiting friends in the congregation and was called on for an impromptu word. Right in the middle of his testimony, he paused. "Five years ago I dedicated my life to Christ," he said. "It was at a youth rally in Newark at which your pastor preached. I've never met your pastor personally till tonight." How elated the pastor was, to learn how God had used him on that earlier occasion.

Because of the unconscious element in influence, we are often unaware of the impact our lives have made. Sometimes months, even years, go by before we learn how something we said or did swayed a soul toward God. But sometime, somewhere, we shall make this happy discovery. One of heaven's serendipities will be finding out how, unknown to us at the time, we were used by God to bless a life.

For example, our Lord foretold the surprise that

will be registered in the Day of Judgment by those who will be honored for treating Christ kindly. Perplexed, they will ask when it was they saw Him hungry and fed Him, thirsty and gave Him drink, a stranger and took Him in, naked and clothed Him, sick or in prison and visited Him. Then the Lord will answer that inasmuch as they did it to the one of the least of His brethren, they did it to Him (Matt. 25:37-40).

Many a cup of cold water has been given in Jesus' name without the giver realizing how refreshing it was. In the day when rewards are meted out, sudden delight will envelop not only worthy saints, but surprised ones as well.

Sudden Conversions

Many persons have begun a day, never expecting that by sunset the direction of their lives would be drastically altered. The first chapter of John mentions several who met Jesus Christ in the span of two days: two disciples of John the Baptist, one of whom was Andrew; then Peter, brought by Andrew; Philip; and Nathanael, brought by Philip. These five never dreamed on the morning of their eventful day that they would dramatically meet the Messiah, the Promised One of Israel.

The woman of Samaria never imagined that as she went to draw water from the well, she would meet the One who would quench the spiritual thirst burning in her soul. Nor that He would make her a witness to the citizens of Samaria to come see a man, who told her all things that she ever did proclaiming Him the Christ (John 4:29).

Neither did the woman, caught in the act of adultery, visualize in her wildest fancy that she would hear the Messiah forgive her with these gracious words, "Neither do I condemn thee; go, and sin no more" (John 8:11).

What a surprise Zaccheus received on that memorable day in which he started out rich, but ended up poor after making fourfold restitution to those he had defrauded. Hearing Jesus was passing through Jericho, he climbed a tree to get a glimpse of Him. Zaccheus had no intention of meeting Christ. But Jesus stopped under the tree, looked up, and invited Himself to Zaccheus' house. Zaccheus was startlingly found by Jesus (Luke 19:1-6).

When the repentant thief was cruelly impaled on the Roman gibbet that Good Friday morn, little did he realize that before noon he would come to believe in the Victim on the middle cross, and would hear Him say, "Today shalt thou be with Me in paradise" (Luke 23:43). What a glorious, unforeseen reversal— to start the day as a condemned thief without hope in this life or in the world to come, and to end it with Christ in paradise!

Puzzling over Old Testament Scripture on his way home from the Passover at Jerusalem, the Ethiopian must have been astonished when a stranger joined him, explained the passage, led him to trust Jesus Christ, and then baptized him. "When they were come up out of the water, the Spirit of the Lord caught away Philip that the eunuch saw him no more: and he went on his way rejoicing" (Acts 8:39). What unanticipated bliss!

The Philippian jailor, one minute in terror, thinking the prisoners had escaped and his life would be therefore forfeited, moments later was on his knees asking the way of salvation. Then an hour or so later, as a new believer, he washed the prisoners' backs, soothed their stripes, provided food for their bodies, and was baptized with the rest of his household. No wonder he rejoiced; his terror was gone! (Acts 16:27-34)

Probably the most dramatic conversion of the early church involved the transformation of the zealot Saul into the Apostle Paul. At one second, he was a self-righteous Pharisee on the Damascus Road, so zealous that he had traveled 100 miles to harass followers of Jesus. The next moment he was groveling in the dust, blinded by a brilliant sun, calling Jesus "Lord," and offering to do His bidding. A few days later he preached in the synagogue in the very town whose believers he had come to persecute, proclaiming that very name he had so vehemently blasphemed (Acts 9). Pauline serendipity.

How many have gone to a church service, or youth rally, or evangelistic crusade, with no deep interest in the Gospel, but who, when brought face-to-face with Jesus Christ, have left the meeting to walk a different road?

C.S. Lewis titled the story of his conversion, *Surprised by Joy.* It happened on the way to a zoo. He was riding in the sidecar of a motorcycle driven by his brother. At the start of the trip he did not believe in the deity of Christ. Somewhere along the way, without any blinding by the noonday sun as in the case of Paul—he found himself believing what he thought he never could.

A lady went to a Sunday evening service to hear a

special speaker. She planned to go from the service to a funeral parlor to pay her respects to a close friend who had passed away. To her own amazement, when she stepped out of the row into the aisle during the invitation, instead of walking to the rear to go outside, she walked to the front to make her decision for Christ.

She said, "By every rule of logic I should have gone out, for the service was long, and I was already late for the viewing. But something propelled me forward. What joy was mine that night! Life has been different since."

A drunken derelict, Joe Killigrew, stepped into a door near New York Times Square to get shelter from the rain. Invited inside, he found himself in the Jerry McAuley Cremorne Mission. A few nights later he accepted Christ, finding forgiveness for his sins and deliverance from alcoholism. Two years later, on the very anniversary of his conversion, he was appointed superintendent of the mission. For nearly a decade he ministered to the down-and-outers. At his funeral service, a close associate estimated that Mr. Killigrew had led 9,000 people to Christ. The night that he stepped into the mission to escape the downpour, Joe Killegrew had no idea of the wonderful blessings in store for him.

Perhaps as you began reading these pages, you had no thought of becoming a Christian. But this meditation has confronted you with your need to trust Christ. Right now the serendipity of salvation can be yours.

10 The Joy of Jesus

No record of Jesus laughing appears in the Bible. On the other hand, the Gospels do tell us that He wept. He was "a Man of sorrows and acquainted with grief" (Isa. 53:3). Many conclude that Jesus exuded gloom wherever He went.

But to think of Jesus only as a man of sorrow is to possess an unbalanced view. Though the Passion Week was a sorrowful time, sorrow was not characteristic of Christ's three-year public ministry. He repeatedly talked about such concepts as *joy, cheer, merriness, gladness,* and *rejoicing.* Before the melancholy days were the sunny months. He was indeed glad as well as sad.

Even at the climax of that foreboding, final week, Jesus was joyful. On the way to Gethsemane, He told His disciples, "These things have I spoken unto you, that My joy might remain in you, and that your joy might be full" (John 15:11). In the Garden He prayed,

"And now I come to Thee; and these tidings I speak in the world, that they might have My joy fulfilled in themselves (John 17:13).

Christ had the Spirit without limit. Since joy is a fruit of the Spirit, Christ must have been a very joyful person. Because the Messiah was anointed . . . with the oil of gladness above His fellows, would He not deserve distinction as the happiest Man that ever lived? (Ps. 45:7) Though no one ever descended to such depths of sorrow as Christ, neither did any one ever climb to such heights of joy.

Things That Did Not Produce His Joy

Material things. Christ possessed few things of joy. When He began His public ministry, He depended partly on the financial support of faithful women (Luke 8:2-3). His disciples weren't wealthy either. They plucked corn on the Sabbath to satisfy their hunger—because they had few coins in their common treasury. The practice of permitting the hungry to pick standing corn was part of a Jewish program for the poor.

Jesus did not even have money on hand to pay His taxes. When the tax collector asked Peter for his Master's tax, the Lord directed Peter to catch a fish, which miraculously had a coin in its mouth (Matt. 17:27).

Christ was born in a borrowed stall, fed the 5,000 with a borrowed lunch, used another's donkey to ride into Jerusalem, borrowed a room for His last supper, died with no possessions, and was buried in a borrowed tomb.

Though rich in heaven, our Lord lived in poverty

on earth so that He might give us spiritual wealth. The source of our Lord's joy was not found in material possessions.

Physical enjoyment. Jesus knew what it was to hunger and thirst. He became so weary that He fell asleep in a violent storm. His disciples, though seasoned sailors of the Sea of Galilee, woke Him up because they feared for their lives.

The Lord spent many a night on the mountaintop in the open air. He cautioned would-be disciples to count the cost of following Him. "The foxes have holes, and the birds of the air have nests; but the Son of Man hath no where to lay His head" (Matt. 8:20).

Jesus did not find joy in pampering His body, nor by indulging in creature comforts.

Human relationships. Jesus was lonely much of the time. His home-town friends misunderstood Him. When He preached in Nazareth, His former neighbors interrupted His sermon and tried to push Him over a precipice. His own brothers did not believe in Him until after the Resurrection.

His disciples frequently failed to understand Him. "O slow of heart" was the way Jesus often addressed them. Many lessons were not grasped till weeks or months later. Though the Lord had repeatedly urged them to humility, the night before He died, they wrangled in the Upper Room over who would be greatest in the kingdom. He told them often that He would rise from the dead, but news of His resurrection was disregarded by some. Many of His professed followers became deserters. Even on the night of arrest, His disciples forsook Him and fled. One betrayed Him.

Though Jesus surely derived some measure of joy from human companionship, the main wellspring was not in human relationships.

Human praise, position, or power. This list of sources from which Christ did not derive his joy is expandable. His joy did not depend on the people's praise. Though at times people said, "He doeth all things well," on other occasions they sought to trap Him in His words, and plotted to take His life. People did shout "Hosannah," but some of the same ones cried a few days later, "Crucify Him."

Our Lord also didn't derive joy from a position of power. By His condescension in the Incarnation, with Master becoming servant, and Life consenting to death, He surrendered all the rights to control and authorize. Perhaps herein lies His secret of joy.

Where Did His Joy Come From?

His jubilation issued from a right relationship with God. No shadow ever crossed between Him and His Father's face. He said, "The Father hath not left Me alone; for I do always those things that please Him" (John 8:29). He kept the channels of communication to heaven open at all times.

In addition, the joy of Christ consisted in the actual doing of the Father's will. "His commandments are not grievous" (l John 5:3), and in the "keeping of them there is great reward" (Ps. 19:ll). At Christ's entrance into the world, He said, "Lo, I come to do Thy will, O God" (Heb. 10:9).

In the Old Testament, animals did not offer themselves voluntarily for sacrifice, but were forced to the slaughter. Yet Christ was a willing sacrifice. Never once did He swerve from His task. The night before He died, He prayed, "Thy will be done" (Matt. 26:42).

Basically, Christ's joy came as a result of obedience, by saying and doing only those things prescribed by His Father. This joy, which enabled Him to endure the cross, carried Him through to the ultimate victory of His mission, the redemption of a numberless host.

Evidences of Jesus' Joy

Despite profound elements of grief and tragedy in His life, Jesus' usual outlook was certainly not morose nor ascetic, but joyful.

He took delight in common joys. Christ did not condemn the common joys of life. Rather, He reveled in the beauties of nature: sheep, flowers, birds, skies, and fields. He delighted in the company of children.

Believing that Christ was a smiling Saviour, the founder of Forest Lawn Cemetery in California searched in vain for a statue of the smiling Christ. When he consulted Italy's greatest sculptors, they replied that Christ did not smile but suffered with the burden of His mission.

Then one sculptor invited him to his studio where he unveiled a rough wood frame, enclosing Jerace's *Christ and the Children.* This original piece is displayed today at Forest Lawn. Though not a smiling Christ, the statue was one to whom children came. Children don't flock to a sour, sad demeanor. Christ must have been bright and cheerful.

He was a popular dinner guest. Jesus accepted newly-converted Matthew's invitation to a feast where publicans and sinners were present in large numbers. Pharisees invited Him to dinner too. He readily entered into the common joys of dining with people. The enjoyable relaxation of such fellowship often provided Him with the proper opportunity to give spiritual instruction (Matt. 9:9-13; Luke 7:36; ll:37; 14:1-24).

In fact, His happy nature and His exuberant participation in such festivities earned Him the reputation among His enemies as "a man gluttonous, and a wine-bibber," a charge completely out of character for anyone who exuded gloom (Matt. ll:19). Though not intemperate, He was a pleasure to have around, a genuinely social person.

Christ's first miracle was performed at a wedding. Solemn people, upon hearing of the shortage of refreshment, would have reacted, "We've had enough gaiety for one day. Let's practice self-discipline and all go home." But Jesus enacted a miracle to keep the party going.

Christ often presented the Gospel with the figure of a feast, as in the parable of the wise and foolish virgins (Matt. 25:1-13). One of the church ordinances, *the Lord's Supper*, was instituted at the "Last Supper." Jesus' final invitation before the Ascension was, "Come and dine" (John 21:12). At His Second Coming, we will celebrate the Marriage Supper of the Lamb with Him (Rev. 19:7).

Comparing the Gospel to a supper suggests joyful fellowship. But if asked what Christianity was all about, most unchurched people would rarely answer in terms of a banquet. People generally consider Christianity solemn, dull, narrow, and a matter of long faces, black prayer books, and dark clothes. But Christ likened Christianity to a feast.

Jesus defended His disciples for not fasting. The Pharisees criticized the disciples because they didn't look gloomy like the staid followers of John the Baptist. Jesus replied that His presence required joy, just as when a bridegroom joins a wedding party (Luke 5:33-34). The Lord forbade hypocritical sadness (Matt. 6:16). His cheerful countenance must have contrasted sharply with the long faces of the rigid Pharisees.

He attracted people from all ranks of life. From the upper levels came Nicodemus, Joanna, the wife of Herod's treasurer, and Joseph of Arimathea. From the middle class came fishermen, soldiers, lawyers. From the lower rungs came despised tax collectors and Samaritans who urged Him to stay in their territory (John 4:40).

What a spectacle it must have been to see this motley group trailing Jesus through the streets and countrysides! A radiant buoyancy must have emanated from Him in order to draw disciples so readily. Crowds who lost Him momentarily were overjoyed to find Him again.

His social camaraderie made Him a welcome guest in many homes. Not only did He weep with those that wept, but also He rejoiced with those that rejoiced. Laughter did not stop when He crossed the threshold. Not only was He a "Man of sorrows acquainted with grief," but also a Man of joy acquainted with fellowship.

Jesus had a sunny disposition. He saw the bright side of things. When He told His disciples He would die,

He also added that He would rise again, and that they would be reunited with Him (John 16:16). At the Last Supper He promised that they would all sup together in the Father's kingdom.

His sunny disposition dispelled shadows and spread cheer wherever He went. The lame man wept for joy! The healed leper, who had lived in a cemetery outside the city, returned home to his family. Peter's mother-in-law, cured of her nagging fever, thankfully rose to minister to those in the house! Because of Christ's healing touch, the blind man for the first time saw the splendors of nature and the faces of his family. The woman, bent over for 18 years, straightened up at the command of Christ and joyfully glorified God!

Many of Christ's expressions command joy directly or indirectly. "Be of good cheer." "Fear not." "Peace be to you." "Let not your heart be troubled." "Blessed are ye." Perhaps we could catch more of His brightness of spirit if we translated the beatitudes, "Happy, happy, happy . . ."

When Christ warned those who laughed that they would later mourn and weep, He was referring to those who laughed derisively at others' misfortunes, or crowed boastfully over evil acts (Luke 6:25). He did promise a reversal of status for His own who wept because of trouble. "Blessed are ye that weep now for ye shall laugh" (6:21).

His joy flowed, not only through His healing prowess, but also through His ability to spiritually uplift. Zaccheus joyfully received Christ into his home. And the Samaritan woman was so overjoyed that she forgot her water pot. Then before His death, Christ promised His disciples a Comforter like Himself. After His resurrection, He brought jubilation to Mary, who was weeping at the tomb.

His joy is reflected in many of the parables. The discovery of the true treasure of life yields joy. The three parables of Luke 15, involving the findings of the lost sheep, coin, and son, reveal the joy of the heavenly Father's heart at the repentance of sinners.

The reward for faithful employment of talents is "the joy of the Lord" (Matt. 13:44; Luke 15:5-7, 9-10, 22-24, 32; Matt. 25:21, 23).

He was thankful, serene, poised, even singing in the face of personal tribulation. For Jesus, gratitude and joy were closely related. Before feeding the 5,000 and the 4,000, Jesus offered thanks for the food. Luke says Jesus was "full of joy" as He praised the Father for hiding spiritual truths from the so-called wise and revealing them to the simple (10:21, NIV).

Midst all the plans of His enemies to kill Him, Jesus maintained His poise. Alert to self-preservation, He withdrew, but did not flee in panic. His retirement was graced with majestic calm.

He possessed a wholesome outlook on life, a freedom from the bondage of legalism. The narrow-minded Pharisees objected to Christ's healing on the Sabbath. But He saw the inconsistency of His critics—on the Sabbath they would unhesitatingly rescue a sheep from a pit, but they didn't want sick people to be healed—at least not on the Sabbath. Christ proceeded to heal on the Sabbath despite their anger.

The night before His death, after instituting the Lord's Supper, He sang a hymn with His disciples (Matt. 26:30). Though things looked desperate, He maintained His optimism. His cousin and forerunner, John the Baptist, had been beheaded. His brothers had turned against Him, thinking He was mad. His crowds had dwindled. Soon His disciples would forsake Him and flee. Then He would be arrested, scourged, mocked, and crucified. Yet He told His disciples not only of His own joy, but also of the fullness of joy that no one can rob from its glad possessor (John 15:11; 16:22, 24).

The Man of Sorrows left us a legacy of joy. He came to give the more abundant life. Though we indeed know the seriousness of life, which tinges joy with gravity; yet for that reason joy is deep, wide, and enduring.

11 We All Need a High

When life gets rough because of disappointment or tragedy, people need something to lift them out of their depression. Or if life just drags on in boredom, they need an outside power to buoy up their spirits.

For centuries man has tried to achieve this high through drugs or other mystical experiences. John Greenleaf Whittier's hymn, *Dear Lord and Father of Mankind,* is the concluding five-stanza section of a seventeen-stanza poem titled, "The Brewing of Soma," which deals with mankind's efforts to attain a religious high.

The first seven stanzas graphically depict pagan priests in India brewing a drug called *Soma,* which they later worshiped, and which caused its imbibers to feel they were soaring elatedly toward the very gates of paradise.

The middle five stanzas review the various attempts through history to induce highs—by music, incense, vigils, trances, sadistic scourgings, dances, or living the cloistered lives of monks. A warning is sounded against the modern-day tendency to seek thrills through aesthetic feelings rather than from true reverence that springs out of the genuine Christian heart—knowledge of Christ.

The poem shifts its focus in the final five-verse portion, used as a hymn. This begins with an admission of our history of folly, "Dear Lord and Father of mankind, forgive our foolish ways," and calls for the joy that comes from a simple following of Christ.

Today millions all over the world turn to drugs, especially alcohol, for a high. Though "spirits" seem to elevate those in low moods, alcohol's damaging effects are well-known. Skeptic Aldous Huxley wrote an essay entitled, "Wanted, a New Pleasure," in which he suggested that the only possible new pleasure, as far as he could see, would be in the discovery of a new drug which would provide a harmless replacement for alcohol. If he were a millionaire, he would finance research for the ideal intoxicant that would abolish inferiority, fill us with love for our fellow men, make life seem divinely beautiful, and enable us to wake up the morning after without any hangover or damaged constitution. In his opinion, such a substitute would solve our problems and make earth a paradise (*Music at Night*, Doubleday & Co., 1930-1, p. 227).

Such a stimulant has been provided by the Christian faith. Paul urged, "Be not drunk with wine, wherein is excess; but be filled with the Spirit" (Eph. 5:18). People under the influence of drugs or alcohol often do things, wrong things, that they would not normally do. In contrast, we Christians are to be under the influence of the Holy Spirit, who will make us act differently from our usual behavior. This verse could be paraphrased, "If you wish zest in your life, do not look for it in wine, but in the inspiration of the Spirit."

Remarkably, references to wine and the Spirit are frequently found in the same context. The Old Testament priest was not to touch strong drink, but to be anointed with oil, which is a type of the Holy Spirit (Lev. 10:7-11). In the New Testament, the crowd at Pentecost thought the apostles were drunk with wine. But they had been baptized with the Holy Spirit (Acts 2:13ff).

The angel said to Zacharias of his son, John the Baptist, "He . . . shall drink neither wine nor strong drink; and he shall be filled with the Holy Ghost, even from his mother's womb" (Luke 1:15).

A professional baseball pitcher, in a drunken spree, caused $1,000 worth of damage to a New York hotel a few years ago. The next season, after his conversion, he went out preaching the Gospel.

Dr. Donald Grey Barnhouse once wrote an article, "Lessons from Drunkenness," in which he contrasted the effects of false joy with those of genuine joy. The Apostle Paul also listed some of the consequences of genuine or Spirit-produced joy.

Song
Strong drink produces pseudo-joy. Who hasn't heard loud, off-key singing coming from some bar or office party, from men and women who would otherwise never sing in public? But under the influence of spirits, they emit artificial joy.

Just as wine produces song, so does the Holy Spirit. In the verse following the command to be Spirit-filled, Paul wrote, "Speaking to yourselves in psalms and hymns and spiritual songs, singing and making melody in your heart to the Lord" (Eph. 5:19).

For the noisy revelers at Ephesus Paul had this advice: Instead of resorting to drugs or wine, throw open your hearts to the Holy Spirit and seek His joy. Then instead of bellowing out some bacchanalian ballad, you will sing from a heart filled with genuine melody to the Lord. Spiritproduced joy gives a lilt and a lift.

Every great revival has been accompanied by singing. Luther's reformation spread through Germany through the humming of hymns by the peasants. Evangelists' names are often associated with the names of their song leaders, like Moody and Sankey, or Graham and Barrows.

Three ministers were eating in a New York City restaurant. In a relaxed mood they were telling jokes and laughing heartily. Nearby sat an actress, whose curiosity finally got the better of her. She leaned over and whispered to one of them, "Pardon me, but aren't you gentlemen clergymen?" When they nodded affirmatively, she continued, "Then tell me. Did you have anything?"

How misguided we are when we think anyone who is cheerful must be imbibing. The joy of the Lord brings genuine song.

Thankfulness

One winter afternoon a snowstorm prevented a plane from taking off on its scheduled flight from Williamsport, Pa. to Newark, NJ. A Christian, ticketed for that flight, overheard the pilot say, "I just flew this plane in from Pittsburgh. The turbulence as I aproached Williamsport was the worst I've experienced since flying over the Himalayas!"

Only two other passengers were waiting for that plane. One said, "I can't think of getting on board in this weather unless I have a drink under my belt." By the time the storm ended and the plane took off at 9 PM, both men were quite happily under the influence.

When the plane landed after a fairly smooth flight, the two men headed toward the cockpit instead of the exit. The Christian watched for a moment, thinking their condition made them walk in the wrong direction. But to his amazement and chagrin, he heard them express an enthusiastic thanks to the pilot for a safe trip. Thought the Christian, "These men did under the influence of drink what I should have done under the control of the Holy Spirit."

The second verse after the command to be filled with the Spirit enjoins, "Giving thanks always for all things unto God" (Eph. 5:20). The joy of the Spirit makes us thankful.

Affability
Though consuming liquor can make a person ugly, hostile, and mean, it often produces agreeability. The cocktail before the party is supposed to create a spirit of goodwill and affability.

One night a preacher was waiting for his wife at a busy corner. He watched as two slow-moving cars skidded on the wet pavement. The cars hit each other, not with much force, but with enough momentum to crumple the grilles into the fronts of the engines. The preacher expected an argument. But to his amazement, the two inebriated drivers stumbled out, looked at the damage, threw their arms around each other and exclaimed, "No harm done!"

Then the preacher imagined two deacons on their way to mid-week meeting whose cars collided in the same kind of accident. He pictured the two deacons emerging from their cars, throwing their arms around each other, and exclaiming, "No harm done!" Just then, commented the preacher, "My imagination said, 'Stop it—you're killing me.'"

The next verse in the series of exhortations after the command to be filled with the Spirit is, "Submitting yourselves one to another in the fear of the Lord" (Eph. 5:21). The joy of the Spirit makes for humility, unity, agreeability, and love. If this joy had held sway in the hearts of the two Philippian women at odds with each other, they would have been able to resolve their differences (Phil. 4:2).

Courage

We call alcoholic beverages "spirits" because alcohol gives a person courage, even though it's false courage. Wine takes a man of inferiority and makes him think he is a superior individual. A person can be himself one minute, then through drink can imagine himself to be a man of distinction, like Napoleon Bonaparte or William the Conqueror.

Wine encourages people to say or do things they would never normally say or do. The intoxicated man enlarges his story, debates, repeats, and begins it all over again. One singer told of a fellow performer who, to get courage to face the audience, drank four bottles of beer before each performance. Another performer, who jumped into a small pool from a high diving board, freely admitted he needed a drink to give him courage before each leap.

The Japanese describe the phases of intoxication by using various animals. The drinker who parades proudly is rooster-drunk. After a bit more booze, when he capers foolishly, he is monkey-drunk. Then as a pig-drunk, he wallows filthily. But the climax comes when he is lion-drunk—then he roars courageously.

The Spirit's joy can give courage in the spiritual realm. This is how men of faith "subdued kingdoms . . . stopped the mouths of lions, quenched the violence of fire, escaped the edge of the sword, out of weakness were made strong, waxed valiant in fight, [and] turned to fight the armies of the aliens" (Heb. 11:33-34).

Genuine joy can loosen our tongues and give us holy boldness. After three years of constant association with Jesus, Peter denied Him three times in one night, even swearing that he did not know Jesus. But seven weeks later this same Peter boldly confessed Christ before thousands of his countrymen. What changed cowering Peter into a courageous preacher? Not only had he seen the risen Christ, but also the Holy Spirit had filled his heart. Genuine joy had given him boldness.

Later, ordered by the authorities not to preach or teach in the name of Jesus, Peter replied that he would obey God rather than men. On release from his arrest, he returned to the church to report what had happened to him. "When they had prayed, the place was shaken . . . and they were all filled with the Holy Ghost, and they spake the Word of God with boldness" (Acts 4:8, 19-20, 31).

The joy of the Lord provided the apostles with strength to carry the Gospel everywhere. Just before His ascension the Lord Jesus promised, "But ye shall receive power, after that the Holy Ghost is come upon you; and ye shall be witnesses unto Me both in Jerusalem, and in all Judea, and in Samaria, and unto the uttermost part of the earth" (Acts 1:8).

When Paul was being transported to Rome as a prisoner, he had every reason to be apprehensive. He was to stand trial before infamous and unpredictable Nero. Potentially, Paul was just around the corner from death. When he came to the Three Taverns, just a few miles south of Rome, what gave him courage was not wine, but the fellowship of like-minded believers who came down from the capital to meet him (Acts 28:15).

Under the joy of the Spirit, a man may act far differently than normal. He can have a song when otherwise he would be sad, be courageous when usually he would be afraid, or show kindness when typically he would react with resentment.

Back in the Prohibition era, a young comedian named Happy Mac made friends with the barkers for the burlesque shows on Chicago's South State Street. He had eight friends in particular, including his special pal, whom he called Big Jim. A middle-aged, six-foot tall, big-boned fellow with a heavily lined face, Big Jim used to bark outside a burlesque, "Come in and see the girlies! You're just in time for the next show!"

When Happy Mac and his eight friends were together, Big Jim would lean over and with real menace in his voice say, "We've got to do something about that Pacific Garden Mission. We lost another one of our show girls to them last week. She went in the mission, got converted, and quit her job. It's unhealthy for our business to have that mission right in the same block."

Happy Mac would change the subject, for he didn't want his friends to know that he had been visiting the mission. But the night of May 29, 1925 after weeks of resistance, Happy Mac, a successful dancer and comedian, received Christ as his Saviour. He experienced real joy within. Soon, he was leading singing at the Pacific Garden Mission.

Afraid of what his friends would say, Happy Mac avoided them for a few weeks. But one night he walked down South State Street. Big Jim was barking away, "Come in and see the pretty girls." Then, seeing Happy Mac, he broke off. "Well, if it ain't little Reverend Happy Mac. Happy, say it's a lie. Say it ain't true that them mission people got my old pal."

Happy Mac replied, "No, it isn't a lie. I've become a Christian." Big Jim wouldn't hear any more. He warned, "Some of us boys might drop in on you some night."

Sure enough that very night when Happy Mac led the singing, Big Jim stood outside the big window, flapping his arms, mimicking Happy Mac's every move. Happy Mac's normal reaction would have been anger. But the fact that he carried on with his song-leading proved that he had been truly changed by the Lord Jesus from the old hot-tempered Happy the boys had known.

A few days later Happy Mac was walking down South State Street, wearing a new tan suit and new shoes, when suddenly all eight friends loomed in front of him, lined up four on each side. As Happy Mac walked between them, they all spat tobacco juice on Happy Mac's new clothes. Unlike the Happy of old, he responded pleasantly, "Your aim's excellent, Jim. Caught my new trousers and shoes."

"That's all you got to say?" Big Jim growled.

"Not quite. There's this. When you get to know Jesus Christ the way I've come to know Him, you'll be able to unclench your fists. You'll let a guy spit on you, and it'll be all right."

Three weeks later Big Jim walked into the mission. "You're not mad at me?" he asked Happy.

"The Lord won't let me get mad any more."

"Happy, have you been a Christian long enough to know how to lead a guy to Jesus?"

When Happy assured him he had, Big Jim said, "Then I'm your customer." That night Big Jim accepted Christ. His change of heart was due to a letter he had received telling him that his mother was dying. He had promised her he would become a Christian before she died. He was able to visit his mother with the good news before her death.

Two weeks later, Big Jim was back on the street, barking again. But instead of inviting people to see a burlesque show, he stood in front of the Pacific Garden Mission, urging people to come in to find forgiveness. Then a few weeks later, Big Jim suddenly dropped dead on the sidewalk. Said Happy Mac, "I thank God for the day Jim spat on my tan suit and new shoes. What if I had lost my temper, as I used to before Christ came into my heart, and before His Spirit controlled my life?"

If we yield to the control of the Holy Spirit, we will possess a real joy that will give us a song. It will also make us thankful, affable, bold, and spiritually strong enough to live for Him. Then we won't need the wrong kind of spirits, for the joy of the Lord will be our high.

Christians, of all people, should live on a high level of joy at all times. In a novel an organist became perturbed with the melancholy subjects used by his pastor Sunday after Sunday. After one unusually gloomy message, the organist impulsively put aside the planned postlude and pealed forth the "Hallelujah Chorus" with such volume that the congregation caught on to his point.

English preacher R.W. Dale wrote, "We ask God to forgive us for our evil thoughts and evil temper, but rarely, if ever, ask Him to forgive us for our sadness."

12 The Lost Chord

Seated at the console of an organ in the evening twilight, a lady let her fingers wander idly over the keys. Though not playing anything in particular, she suddenly struck one chord which sounded like a great amen at the close of an angel's psalm.

It quieted pain and sorrow,
Like love overcoming strife;
It seemed the harmonious echo
From our discordant life.

(Adelaide Anne Proctor, "The Lost Chord," in *The World's Great Religious Poetry*, ed. Caroline Miles Hill, The MacMillan Co., 1945, p. 577).

The chord faded away into silence as though it were loathe to leave. But try as she did to find again that chord which seemed to come from the very soul of the organ, it was lost.

This story reminds us of the lost joy of some Christians. At the start of their Christian lives, they struck

117

the chords of delightful lives. These notes brought heaven to earth. But somehow through the years, these notes dwindled into silence, leaving them to ask,

> Where is the blessedness I knew
> When first I saw the Lord?

Joy Can Be Lost

A man invariably ended his prayer during prayer time at the midweek meeting this way,

> Some are sick; some are sad;
> And some have lost the joy they had.

When the Israelites longed for meat in their wilderness journey, the Lord "gave them their request; but sent leannesss into their soul" (Ps. 106:15). The Prophet Isaiah, speaking of divine judgment to come, warned that joy would disappear (Isa. 24:7-8, 11).

Jeremiah prophesied, "Then will I cause to cease from the cities of Judah, and from the streets of Jerusalem, the voice of mirth, and the voice of gladness, the voice of the bridegroom, and the voice of the bride" (Jer. 7:34). He also predicted that joy and gladness would be taken from Moab (48:33). Likewise, Ezekiel foretold the ceasing of the sound of songs and harps in Tyre (Ezek. 26:13). Hosea gave similar warnings (Hosea 2:11).

Removal of joy has been part of God's judgment on those who depart from His way. Warnings against Judah were fulfilled in the Exile. As captives in a foreign country, the Israelites sat down by the rivers of Babylon and wept, hanging their harps on willows. When asked to sing one of the songs of Zion, they answered in this manner "How shall we sing the

Lord's song in a strange land?" (Ps. 137:1-4)

Vivid memories of past blessings contrasted with one's present predicament can cause the song to disappear. The prodigal son, feeding on the husks left by the swine, was miserable as he thought of past delights in his father's house where even the servants were better off than he.

The restoration after the Exile restored the Israelites' song. They joined in joyfully, "When the Lord turned again the captivity of Zion, we were like them that dream. Then was our mouth filled with laughter, and our tongue with singing: then said they among the heathen, 'The Lord hath done great things for . . . us; whereof we are glad'" (Ps. 126:1-3).

At the laying of the temple's foundation, the priests led a praise service. Accompanied by trumpets and cymbals, "they sang together by course in praising and giving thanks unto the Lord; because He is good, for His mercy endureth forever. . . . And all the people shouted with a great shout, when they praised the Lord" (Ezra 3:11).

But even that joy was tempered by the memory of Solomon's glorious temple. Many of the "ancient men, that had seen the first house, when the foundation of this house was laid before their eyes, wept with a loud voice; and many shouted aloud for joy; so that the people could not discern the noise of the shout of joy from the noise of the weeping" (vv. 12-13). These same foundations are the site of the historic Wailing Wall.

Reasons for Loss of Joy

Israel was warned that despising God's commands

would result in "sorrow of heart" (Lev. 26:16). When Jeremiah threatened absence of joy, he gave the reason, "'Because our fathers have forsaken Me,' saith the Lord, 'and have walked after other gods . . . and have not kept My law'" (Jer. 16:11). Since the believer's joy stems from walking certain avenues, if he neglects to walk these paths, joy will flee.

For example, you used to rise early or set apart definite periods to meditate in the Word. But something has crept in, so that you seldom read your Bible now. Abandonment of a practice that brings inner rejoicing will soon remove the joyous burning of the heart.

You used to have a quiet time when you worshiped God in adoration, and besought Him with supplication, but you no longer have a prayer life. The lost chord of prayer brings decreasing joy.

You scarcely attend church any more. Thus, you lose the elation that comes from joint contemplation of the attributes and works of God. You likewise miss the jubilation springing from fellowship with other believers.

Still another lost chord is that of soul-winning. You used to hand out tracts, or participate in open-air meetings, or even lead others to Christ. But you no longer actively spread the Good News. Joy has declined.

Perhaps you used to have a strong interest in the worldwide spread of the Gospel. You knew missionaries by name, and enjoyed missionary conferences and giving. Other interests have slowly crept in to cut your ardor, also your joy.

David's Lost Joy

Is a hit-and-run driver happy because he escapes detection after deserting his injured victim? Not at all. Often an apprehended lawbreaker exclaims, "I'm glad it's over. No one knows the torture I've been through!"

Guilt stemming from a violation of God's law is real and must be handled. If we try to cover this guilt, we only shove it more deeply within. It will poison us until we confess our sin.

David knew the burden of unconfessed sin. After committing adultery with Bathsheba and learning that she was pregnant, he arranged a furlough for her husband to make it appear that he had fathered the baby. But when her husband returned to the battle-front, after refusing to visit his wife during his leave, David secretly ordered him positioned in a dangerous spot that would result in his death. Thus, David became guilty of murder as well as adultery.

Months went by before David repented. How did he feel during that period? David's penitential psalm (32) gives psychological insight into the havoc caused him by his unconfessed sin. He said, "When I kept silence, my bones waxed old through my roaring all the day long" (v. 3).

Instead of admitting his sin to God, David thrust his wrongdoing into his subconscious. But his sin seeped out in symptoms of physical and mental distress. His body became weak. Grief sapped his energy and strength. Failure to speak upwardly to God caused the transgression to shout inwardly. His smothered sin smoldered within. As a result, David suffered from a psychosomatic illness.

Night brought no relief. Even in sleep he felt the burden. "For day and night Thy hand was heavy upon me; my moisture is turned into the drought of summer" (v. 4). Modern psychologists suggest the language indicated a high fever and dehydration. Parched and barren, he tossed and turned as under a tropical sun. Though silence reigned without, sorrow tormented within. Repressed sin imperiled his health.

Perhaps David excused himself, "I'm human like other people." Or, "I'm a king. I can do as I please. I can marry any woman I want. And I can order any soldier anywhere." But the persistence of inner torture was proof of the inescapableness of God's judgment. David needed forgiveness for his sin.

The Prophet Nathan began to suspect something. Why had David married Bathsheba so soon after Uriah's death? Then when this attractive widow showed signs of advanced pregnancy soon after the wedding, Nathan knew.

The Lord sent Nathan to David. This prophet, who told it like it was, approached David wisely. He asked David's help in solving a sad situation. A rich man with large flocks needed a lamb to prepare for his dinner guest. Instead of taking one of his many animals, he confiscated a poor man's only lamb and family pet, and cooked it.

Perhaps David's fist pounded on the table. "As the Lord liveth, the man that hath done this thing shall surely die" (2 Sam. 12:5). For a few moments Nathan sat still, looking straight into David's eyes. Then with deliberation he stated, "Thou art the man" (v. 7).

David's face turned ashen. After moments of agonized silence, David finally spoke, not as a proud monarch, but as a repentant evildoer, "I have sinned against the Lord" (v. 13).

David's Restored Joy

Then he uttered one of the most graphic, anguished confessions found anywhere in literature. He begged for mercy and for cleansing. Psalm 51 bears the title, "A Psalm of David, When Nathan the Prophet Came unto Him, After He Had Gone in to Bathsheba." His prayer for forgiveness did not go unanswered. David discovered that the depths of his depravity could be surpassed by the marvel of divine mercy. What relief from his inward turmoil!

Twice in his penitential prayer, he asked for the restoration of joy. "Make me to hear joy and gladness; that the bones which Thou hast broken may rejoice. . . . Restore unto me the joy of Thy salvation" (vv. 8, 12). How his heart throbbed with jubilation when the lost chord was revived!

When wrongdoing breaks our fellowship with the Lord, joy disappears (Isa. 59:2). A missionary wrote his professor 12 years after graduation from a Christian college, "I lied about completing all the assignments for your course. I should not have passed. For many years I haven't had the joy I once had." The professor assigned a project which the missionary willingly completed to fulfill graduation requirements. His joy returned.

Peter must have spent a sleepless night after denying his Master so vehemently in the high priest's courtyard. Also, the day of the Crucifixion, and the day after, must have been filled with grief. But on the day of the Resurrection, Christ met with Peter privately. Though no record of the dialogue exists, the first order of business had to be Christ's forgiveness of Peter for his defection. Peter doubtless bubbled with restored joy.

A Christian woman with little joy in her life came across the verse, "Let him that stole steal no more" (Eph. 4:28). She again remembered that she had cheated her brother out of $1500 in a relative's will. She arranged to meet her lawyer and her brother. With tearful confession she gave her brother a check for $1500. But she left with a light heart.

On the other side of the fence, a man, cheated out of his inheritance by a brother, vowed he would never forgive him. Thirty years later he learned his brother, who had lost his wife and only child in an accident, was dying. Stifling pride and hate, he went to see his failing brother. The smile of God met him.

The Church at Ephesus

The Ephesians had turned from idols to serve the living God. Not only was the image-making business dealt a severe blow, but also believers who had been practicing black magic made a public bonfire of their incantation books and charms (Acts 19:18-27). The same enthusiasm which had made them fanatical pagans now transformed them into fervent Christians. Joy enthralled them.

But something happened, perhaps not all at once. The early flush of consecration faded. John wrote, "Thou has left thy first love" (Rev. 2:4). And when their love went, their joy disappeared also. Though commended for their hard work, patience and ortho-doxy, they were loveless and joyless.

How they lost their love and joy we are not told. Perhaps it was because of too much concern over making money, or too much indulgence in pleasure. They didn't keep up their daily devotional time through the Word and prayer. They neglected their personal relationships with Christ, failing to meditate on Gethsemane and Golgotha. Though going through the motions of Christian service, their teaching, sing-ing, and almsgiving had degenerated into formality without love. They had become mechanical.

But the Holy Spirit told them how to regain that first love and lost joy. First, they were to "remember . . . from whence thou art fallen" (v. 4). They were to recall their original delights in self-denial, willingness to sacrifice, zeal to serve, fervor in prayer, and de-tachment from all evil. They were to recollect how they had enjoyed Bible study, the worship services, and helping the poor. They were to admit they had lapsed from one-time warmth, and confess the lost chord in their lives.

Second, told were these believers to repent. Merely lamenting the good old days and loss of fervor wasn't enough. They had to have a change of mind which would result in a change of direction.

Third, they were then to repeat the first works, going back to the kind of Christian life which had characterized their early post-conversion days. For those of us who long to find the lost chord, it will mean reentering those avenues of spiritual joys. It may involve again attending the church services, the midweek meeting, giving out tracts, visitations in hospitals and nursing homes, tithing, assisting the needy, and upholding justice.

A 6-foot, 200-pound football player became pastor of a church. The former pastor for 40 years had never really relinquished leadership of the church—he pulled strings from behind the scenes. One day the ex-football player visited the elderly pastor. Immediately, the former pastor began criticizing the younger man—telling him exactly what he was doing wrong. Then the ex-football player told off the former pastor in choice language.

For many Sundays when the younger pastor preached, nothing happened. No joy was in his heart. No blessing for the people. Then the old pastor moved 100 miles away. The low spiritual ebb continued for weeks. One night the young preacher said to his wife, "Do you suppose it could be my relationship to the former pastor that's causing this lack of joy?" His wife responded, "You know it is."

In the morning the ex-football player drove his old jalopy 100 miles to a rooming house. When the old preacher came to the door, he resumed his tongue-lashing, taking up where he had left off before, listing everything the young pastor was doing wrong. The ex-football player did all he could to hold himself in, silently praying, *Lord, if you ever held a man in check, do it now.*

When the old man finished, the ex-football player simply said, "I'm sorry for what I said to you. I was wrong."

The old pastor immediately uttered, "*I* was wrong." They nearly had an argument over who was wrong. They threw their arms around each other in mutual forgiveness. The old joy returned to the young pastor. Back in his pulpit, the old power surged again.

A little boy was pleased with the card given him in Sunday School titled, "Joy from God." On the bus on his way home, his precious possession slipped from his fingers and fluttered through an open window. The lad called out to the driver, "I've lost my 'Joy from God.' Please stop the bus." The good-natured driver brought the bus to a halt. The little boy climbed out and recovered his "Joy from God."

Travelers on the Christian way who lose the joy of the Lord should first admit it, then pray with David, "Cleanse me from sin, and restore unto me the joy of Thy salvation." Then that lost chord will vibrate once more.